GALVESTON DIET COOKBOOK FOR BEGINNERS

Navigate Your Menopause Through Easy, Nutrient-Rich, Anti-Inflammatory Recipes and Comprehensive Meal Plan with Shopping Lists Designed for Hormonal Balance and Sustainable Weight Loss

Sheryl Thompson

Disclaimer Notice:
Please be advised that the information in this document is intended solely for educational and entertainment purposes. Every effort has been made to ensure that the information provided is complete, accurate, and reliable. There are no warranties, either expressed or implied. Readers recognize that the author is not providing legal, financial, medical, or professional advice. The content of this book has been compiled from a variety of sources. It is recommended that you seek the advice of a licensed professional prior to implementing any of the techniques described in this book.

TABLE OF CONTENTS

CHAPTER 4: EVENING INDULGENCES / 53

CHAPTER 5: HEALTHY SNACK WONDERS / 67

CHAPTER 6: BEVERAGE BLISS / 77

CHAPTER 7: 28-DAYS MEAL PLAN / 83

CONCLUSION / 101

APPENDIX: / 104

MEASUREMENT CONVERSION CHART / 104

DIRTY DOZEN & CLEAN FIFTEEN / 107

CHAPTER 1

INTRODUCTION

"Your body is your most priceless possession… so go take care of it."

- Jack Lalanne -

MAIN PRINCIPLES OF THE GALVESTON DIET

Welcome to the world of the Galveston Diet! If you're here, you're probably looking for a way to feel healthier, more energetic, and maybe even squeeze back into those jeans you've been eyeing in the back of your closet. Well, you've come to the right place. I'm excited to take you on this journey, and trust me, it's going to be more fun and rewarding than you might think.

When I first started the Galveston Diet, I was like many of you—frustrated with the traditional advice of "eat less, move more" and feeling stuck in a cycle of weight gain and low energy. Having experienced the challenges of midlife, I knew something had to change. Discovering the Galveston Diet gave me a renewed sense of hope, like I had finally found the missing piece to a puzzle I'd been struggling with for years.

Overview of the Diet

Let's start with a quick overview of what the Galveston Diet is all about. This isn't just another fad diet or a quick fix. Instead, it's a thoughtfully designed approach that combines intermittent fasting with a focus on anti-inflammatory foods. The diet's core idea is to fuel your body with the right nutrients, while allowing time for it to rest and repair – kind of like giving your car a tune-up but for your insides. We're talking about a plan that's not only sustainable, but also enjoyable.

Now, you might be thinking, "Another diet? Really?" Trust me, I get it. The world is full of diets that promise the moon and deliver, well, maybe a pebble. But the Galveston Diet is different because it was created with women in mind—especially those of us dealing with the ups and downs of midlife.

Introduction to Dr. Mary Claire Haver

Now, let's talk about the brilliant mind behind this diet—Dr. Mary Claire Haver. Dr. Haver is an OB-GYN who hails from Galveston, Texas (yep, that's where the diet gets its name). Like many of us, she found herself frustrated with the traditional advice of "eat less, move more," especially as she noticed it wasn't working for her or her patients who were going through menopause. They were eating salads, skipping desserts, and yet, the scale wouldn't budge. Sound familiar?

Dr. Haver saw firsthand how conventional diets were failing women, particularly those facing the unique challenges of midlife. Women were exhausted, irritable, and feeling defeated by the number on the scale. Determined to find a solution, Dr. Haver dove into research and asked a critical question: "Do menopausal women need a special diet?" Her answer was a resounding yes.

Through her research, Dr. Haver developed the Galveston Diet, a plan that acknowledges and addresses the hormonal and metabolic changes which women experience as they age. This diet isn't about deprivation or obsession with calorie counting; it's about understanding your body, fueling it with the right nutrients, and finding a balance that works for you. Dr. Haver's approach has transformed the lives of countless women, helping them not only lose weight, but also regain their energy, confidence, and zest for life.

The Science Behind the Galveston Diet

So, what makes the Galveston Diet tick? It all boils down to three main principles: intermittent fasting, anti-inflammatory foods, and macronutrient tracking. Let's break these down in a way that's easy to digest (pun intended) and explore the phases that guide you through this transformative journey.

Intermittent Fasting

Don't let the term scare you off. Before you start worrying about skipping meals or feeling deprived, let me clarify. Intermittent fasting isn't about depriving yourself of food; it's about giving your body a break from continuous digestion, so it can prioritize repair and recovery. Think of it as a way to reset your system. The Galveston Diet typically follows a 16:8 fasting schedule, where you fast for 16 hours and eat within an 8-hour window. This method not only helps regulate insulin levels but also promotes fat burning and reduces inflammation. It's like giving your metabolism a gentle nudge in the right direction.

Anti-Inflammatory Foods

Next up, anti-inflammatory foods. These are the unsung heroes of the Galveston Diet. Inflammation is a major player in many chronic diseases and can wreak havoc on your body, especially as you age. By focusing on foods that reduce inflammation—like leafy greens, berries, and fatty fish—you're essentially giving your body the tools it needs to fight back against the negative effects of aging and stress.

Think of these foods as your body's internal peacekeepers, quelling the fires of inflammation and helping you feel more energized and less sluggish. The beauty of the Galveston Diet is that it doesn't just tell you what not to eat; it introduces you to a world of delicious, nutrient-rich foods that support your health in the long term.

Macronutrient Tracking

Finally, there's macronutrient tracking. Now, this might sound a bit technical, but it's really just a way of ensuring you're getting the right balance of fats, proteins, and carbs. Each of these macronutrients plays a crucial role in your body's functioning, and the Galveston Diet helps you find the perfect combination.

Fats are your friends here, particularly healthy fats like those found in avocados, nuts, and olive oil. They help keep you full, support brain health, and even aid in hormone production. Protein is vital for maintaining muscle mass (something we tend to lose as we age), and carbs—yes, carbs! —are included too, but in a way that ensures you're getting the right kinds to fuel your body without spiking your blood sugar.

By paying attention to your macronutrients, you'll be nourishing your body in a balanced way, helping to maintain steady energy levels and prevent those dreaded sugar crashes.

Phases of the Galveston Diet

The Galveston Diet is structured around two main phases that guide you through dietary changes focused on reducing inflammation, promoting fat loss, and improving overall health. Here's a closer look at each phase:

Phase 1: Inflammation Elimination

Phase 1 is all about hitting the reset button on inflammation. The goal here is to significantly cut down on inflammation in your body by eliminating inflammatory foods like processed sugars, refined carbohydrates, and trans fats. Instead, you'll focus on nutrient-dense, anti-inflammatory foods, such as lean proteins, healthy fats, vegetables, and berries. This phase is designed to restore balance and get your body back on track, which helps with weight management and boosts energy levels.

Intermittent fasting is introduced during this phase to help regulate insulin levels and promote fat burning. By combining nutritious, anti-inflammatory foods with intermittent fasting, you're helping your body heal from the inside out. For this first month-long phase, Dr. Haver recommends that each meal consist of 70% healthy fats, 20% lean protein, and 10% carbohydrates. This combination helps to wean you off sugar and processed carbs while encouraging fat-burning.

Phase 2: Fuel Refocus

Once you've completed Phase 1 and your body is feeling more balanced, it's time to move on to Phase 2, where we shift our focus to how you fuel your body. This phase builds on the solid foundation laid in the first phase by fine-tuning macronutrient ratios to fit your individual needs. The emphasis remains on maintaining an anti-inflammatory lifestyle, while allowing for a bit more flexibility in your food choices.

In Phase 2, you'll refine your macronutrient intake to better support sustainable weight loss and overall health. The focus here is on consuming a balanced mix of healthy fats, proteins, and fiber-rich carbohydrates. Specifically, Dr. Haver suggests adjusting your meals to 40% fat, 20% protein, and 40% carbohydrates. This balanced approach helps you maintain long-term habits that support weight maintenance and hormonal balance, while still enjoying a variety of foods.

By the time you reach Phase 2, you'll have developed the habits and knowledge needed to keep things balanced and enjoyable. This phase is all about creating lasting changes that make you feel great while allowing you the flexibility to live your life fully.

When you combine the three principles with a phased approach to dietary changes, you get a powerful, effective, and sustainable approach to health and weight management. The Galveston Diet isn't just about fitting into your jeans (though that's a nice bonus); it's about feeling good in your skin, having the energy to do the things you love, and taking care of your body in a way that's both realistic and enjoyable.

UNDERSTANDING MENOPAUSE AND HORMONAL & METABOLIC CHANGES

Alright, now that we've got a solid overview of the Galveston Diet and its foundation, let's dive into something that's crucial for understanding why this diet works so well—especially if you're navigating the complexities of menopause.

Hormonal Shifts During Menopause

Menopause is a natural phase of life, but it's also one that can come with a lot of changes, both physical and emotional. As mentioned earlier, one of the main drivers behind the Galveston Diet was Dr. Mary Claire Haver's realization that traditional diet advice didn't quite cut it for women experiencing menopause. Why? Because menopause brings about some significant hormonal shifts that can impact everything from your mood to your metabolism.

During menopause, the levels of estrogen and progesterone in your body decrease. These hormones play a crucial role in regulating your menstrual cycle, but they also influence other areas of your health. For example, lower estrogen levels can affect your metabolism, bone density, and even your mood. This can lead to symptoms, like hot flashes, night sweats, and even weight gain, which can feel frustrating and overwhelming.

Think of hormones as the body's little messengers. When they're out of balance, it's like having a bunch of confused GPS signals. Your body's systems might not function as smoothly, leading to issues like stubborn weight gain, disrupted sleep, and changes in mood.

Metabolic Slowdown and Weight Gain

One of the most talked-about changes during menopause is a slowdown in metabolism. As estrogen levels drop, your body's ability to burn calories efficiently can diminish. This can lead to weight gain, particularly around the midsection, which can be discouraging, especially if you feel like you're doing everything "right" in terms of diet and exercise.

This metabolic slowdown doesn't mean your body is broken or that you've somehow failed. It's just a natural part of aging and hormonal shifts. The good news is that there are ways to address this and get back on track.

How the Galveston Diet Addresses These Changes

So, how does the Galveston Diet fit into this picture? As mentioned earlier, this diet is specifically designed to tackle the unique challenges of menopause. Here's how it helps:

Intermittent fasting helps by giving your digestive system a break and allowing your body to switch from burning sugar to burning fat, which can help combat the abdominal fat gain that often accompanies menopause. It also helps regulate insulin levels, which can become more erratic during this time.

The focus on anti-inflammatory foods helps reduce the chronic inflammation that can be exacerbated by hormonal changes. By incorporating foods that fight inflammation, you can help manage symptoms and support overall health, which is crucial when your body is undergoing such significant shifts.

Finally, macronutrient tracking ensures that you're getting a balanced intake of fats, proteins, and carbs. This balance is key for maintaining muscle mass, supporting metabolic health, and keeping your energy levels steady. By focusing on nutrient-dense foods and avoiding processed options, the Galveston Diet helps keep your metabolism running as efficiently as possible.

UNDERSTANDING INTERMITTENT FASTING

Let's discuss one of the core components of the Galveston Diet: intermittent fasting. I know, "fasting" can sound a bit intimidating, like something reserved for monks or extreme dieters. But fear not! Intermittent fasting is more about timing than it is about extreme restrictions, and it can be a powerful tool for improving your overall health.

What is Intermittent Fasting?

Intermittent fasting (IF) is a way of structuring your meals that focuses on when you eat, rather than what you eat. The main idea is simple—you switch between eating and fasting periods. There are a few popular ways to do it, like the 16/8 method, where you fast for 16 hours and eat within an 8-hour window. Another is the 5:2 method, where you eat normally for five days and cut back on calories for two non-consecutive days. There's also the Eat-Stop-Eat method, where you do a 24-hour fast once or twice a week.

Benefits of Fasting

You might be wondering, "What's in it for me?" Fasting offers a range of benefits that can make it an attractive option for those looking to improve their health and well-being. Let's break down some of the key advantages:

1. **Improved Metabolism:** Intermittent fasting can help enhance your metabolism by increasing your body's ability to burn fat for energy. When you fast, your body depletes its glycogen stores and starts to utilize fat stores, which can aid in weight management.

2. **Cellular Repair:** During fasting periods, your body initiates a process called autophagy, where it cleans out damaged cells and regenerates new ones. This process is crucial for maintaining cellular health and longevity.

3. **Better Insulin Sensitivity:** Fasting boosts insulin sensitivity, meaning your body becomes better at utilizing insulin. This can help keep blood sugar levels stable and reduce the likelihood of type 2 diabetes.

4. **Enhanced Mental Clarity:** Many people report increased mental clarity and focus during fasting periods. This could be due to more stable blood sugar levels and the release of brain-derived neurotrophic factor (BDNF), a protein linked to cognitive function.

5. **Simplified Eating Schedule:** Instead of worrying about planning and preparing multiple meals throughout the day, intermittent fasting simplifies your eating schedule. You've got a set eating window, which can make meal planning a bit more straightforward.

How to Start Fasting Safely

Starting an intermittent fasting regimen is like setting up a new routine—there's a bit of an adjustment period, but it's manageable with a little preparation. Here's how to ease into it safely:

1. **Start Gradually:** If the idea of fasting for 16 hours sounds overwhelming, start with a shorter fasting window and gradually increase it. You might begin with 12/12 (12 hours fasting, 12 hours eating) and work your way up to 16/8.

2. **Stay Hydrated:** Water is your ally during fasting. Drink plenty of it to stay hydrated and help curb hunger. Herbal tea, black coffee, and the beverages recipes included in this cookbook are also great options if you need a little variety.

3. **Listen to Your Body:** Pay attention to how you feel. If you experience any adverse effects, such as dizziness or extreme fatigue, consider adjusting your fasting window or consulting with a healthcare provider.

4. **Plan Your Meals:** When you're eating, make sure your meals are balanced and nutrient-dense. Focus on whole foods, including lean proteins, healthy fats, and plenty of vegetables.

Combining Intermittent Fasting with the Galveston Diet

Now, let's connect the dots. The Galveston Diet places a strong emphasis on the 16/8 intermittent fasting method, where you fast for 16 hours and eat during an 8-hour window. This approach aligns perfectly with the diet's goals of improving metabolic health, managing weight, and enhancing overall well-being.

It's worth noting that with this schedule, many followers of the Galveston Diet start eating around noon. So, your breakfast might look more like lunch. And that's perfectly okay! The concept of breakfast is flexible, and you can enjoy «breakfast» foods at any time of day. However, the Galveston Diet tends to focus on more savory options for your first meal, with two meals and two snacks recommended throughout the day.

Here's a sample routine to give you an idea of how a day might look:

- **12:00 PM:** Break your fast with a balanced meal that includes protein, healthy fats, and fiber.

- **3:00 PM:** Enjoy a nutrient-rich snack.

- **6:00 PM:** Have your second meal, focusing on a mix of lean protein, vegetables, and healthy fats.

- **7:45 PM:** A light, satisfying snack to keep you full until your next fasting period begins.

I remember when I first tried intermittent fasting. As someone who's always been passionate about nutrition, I was intrigued but skeptical. I was used to nibbling on snacks throughout the day, convinced that my metabolism needed constant fuel. But once I embraced the 16:8 method, I noticed my energy levels were more stable, and I wasn't constantly thinking about food. It felt like giving my digestive system a mini-vacation every day!

BENEFITS OF THE GALVESTON DIET

The Galveston Diet isn't just another way to eat; it's a comprehensive approach to wellness with several standout benefits:

1. **Weight Management:** By integrating intermittent fasting with a focus on anti-inflammatory foods, the Galveston Diet helps you manage your weight more effectively. It addresses both the hormonal and metabolic changes that can make weight loss challenging in midlife.

2. **Improved Energy Levels:** The diet's emphasis on nutrient-dense foods and balanced macronutrients helps stabilize your energy levels throughout the day. No more afternoon slumps or feeling sluggish—just steady, reliable energy.

3. **Better Hormonal Balance:** With its focus on reducing inflammation and supporting hormonal health, the Galveston Diet can help mitigate some of the symptoms of menopause. It supports hormonal balance, which can lead to fewer mood swings, better sleep, and overall improved well-being.

4. **Enhanced Mental Clarity:** The diet's combination of intermittent fasting and anti-inflammatory foods supports brain health and cognitive function. You'll likely experience better mental clarity, improved focus, and a greater sense of mental well-being.

REASONS TO CHOOSE THE GALVESTON DIET

So, why should you choose the Galveston Diet over other options? Here's why it stands out:

1. **Tailored for Women in Midlife:** This diet is specifically designed to meet the needs of women going through menopause. It addresses the unique hormonal and metabolic changes that come with this stage of life, offering a plan that's both practical and effective.

2. **Focus on Anti-Inflammatory Foods:** The diet emphasizes foods that combat inflammation, which is crucial for reducing menopause-related symptoms and improving overall health. You'll be eating foods that help keep inflammation at bay and support a healthier you.

3. **Sustainable Lifestyle Change:** Unlike fad diets that promise quick fixes, the Galveston Diet is about making lasting changes. It's a sustainable approach that fits into your life and promotes long-term health and well-being.

FOOD TO AVOID, RECOMMENDED FOOD

Alright, let's talk food! Finding the right balance can make all the difference in how you feel and how effective the Galveston Diet can be for you. So, let's dive in and make sure you're armed with all the knowledge you need to make delicious and healthy choices!

Foods to Avoid on the Galveston Diet

Navigating the Galveston Diet means knowing which foods to steer clear of to help you reach your health goals. Some foods can interfere with your progress by contributing to inflammation, disrupting metabolism, or throwing your hormones out of balance. Here's a handy guide to keep you on track and feeling your best.

Sugars and Artificial Sweeteners:

High-sugar foods and artificial sweeteners are a big no-no. They can spike your insulin levels, which disrupts your hormonal balance and often leads to weight gain. Plus, they're usually low in nutrients and can leave you feeling unsatisfied. Here's what to avoid:

- Sugar
- Artificial sweeteners (aspartame, saccharin, sucralose)
- Candy
- Pastries
- Cookies

Fried and Processed Foods:

Fried foods and heavily processed items are notorious for their unhealthy fats, excess sodium, and preservatives. These can lead to inflammation and negatively impact your overall health. Stay away from:

- Fried foods
- Processed foods
- Junk food
- Chips

Refined Grains and Flours:

Refined grains have been stripped of essential nutrients and fiber, causing blood sugar spikes and leaving you feeling hungry soon after eating. Avoid the following:

- White pasta
- Refined grains and flours
- Pizza (especially those with refined flour crusts)

Instead, opt for whole grains to keep your blood sugar levels stable and your meals more satisfying.

Processed Meats:

Processed meats are often loaded with unhealthy fats, sodium, and nitrates, which are linked to increased health risks. For a healthier choice, avoid:
- Processed meats with nitrates (hot dogs, sausages, deli meats) Unhealthy Oils:

Unhealthy Oils:

Certain oils, particularly those high in omega-6 fatty acids, can promote inflammation and mess with the balance of healthy fats in your diet. Steer clear of:

- Vegetable oils (corn, canola, soybean oils)
- Soybean oil
- Sunflower oil
- Safflower oil
- Corn oil
- Canola oil

Foods with Artificial Additives:

Artificial flavors, colors, and preservatives can interfere with your body's natural processes and contribute to health issues. Avoid products that contain:

- Artificial flavors, colors, and preservatives

Alcohol:

While it might be tempting to unwind with a glass of wine or a cold beer, alcohol can disrupt sleep, hormone regulation, and metabolism. It's best to avoid or limit your intake to stay on track with your health goals.

Recommended Foods and Ingredients

On the Galveston Diet, what you put on your plate is just as important as what you leave off. Here's a rundown of the nutrient-packed, inflammation-fighting foods that will keep you satisfied and help you thrive.

Fats:

Healthy fats are essential for maintaining hormone balance, aiding nutrient absorption, and keeping you full. Opt for high-quality, minimally processed fats and oils to support overall health:

- Avocados
- Avocado oil
- Butter (preferably from grass-fed cows)
- Coconut flakes (in moderation)
- Coconut flour (for use in recipes)
- Coconut oil (in moderation)
- Creamy dressing (for use in recipes)
- Dairy fats (heavy cream, full-fat milk), if tolerated
- Flaxseed oil
- Ghee (clarified butter)
- Hummus
- Mayonnaise (made with olive or avocado oil)
- MCT oil (in moderation)
- Nuts (walnuts, almonds, pecans, macadamias); almond flour
- Nut butters (sugar-free and free of added oils)
- Olive oil
- Olives
- Seed butters (sugar-free and free of added oils)
- Seeds (chia, flax, hemp, pumpkin, sunflower)
- Sesame oil (in moderation)
- Tahini (sesame seed butter)

Approved Proteins:

Protein is key for muscle maintenance, metabolism, and overall health. Focus on high-quality proteins from lean meats, fish, and plant-based sources:

- Anchovies
- Bacon (uncured, nitrate-free)
- Beef (lean cuts)
- Beef jerky (nitrate-free)
- Bison
- Buffalo
- Chicken
- Collagen protein powder
- Cornish hens
- Duck
- Eggs
- Fish (wild-caught, especially salmon, trout, and tuna)
- Game (venison)
- Legumes
- Nitrate/nitrite-free deli meats
- Ostrich
- Pork (lean cuts)
- Protein powder (limited ingredient, low sugar, low carbohydrate)
- Shellfish
- Tofu
- Turkey
- Turkey bacon

Vegetable Proteins:

For a plant-based twist, these vegetable proteins are nutrient-dense and versatile:

- Almond milk/cheese/flour
- Cashew milk/cheese
- Chia seeds
- Chickpeas/chickpea flour
- Dried or canned beans
- Edamame
- Hemp hearts/milk
- Lentils
- Lupin beans
- Nutritional yeast
- Seitan
- Tempeh
- Tofu

Approved Dairy Proteins:

Dairy can be a great protein source if you opt for full-fat, minimally processed options:

- Cheddar
- Cottage cheese (full-fat)
- Cream cheese
- Feta cheese
- Goat cheese
- Greek yogurt (full-fat)
- Havarti
- Heavy cream
- Kefir (full-fat)
- Monterey Jack
- Mozzarella and other softer cheeses
- Parmesan and other hard cheeses
- Sour cream
- Swiss

Approved Non-Starchy Vegetables:

These vegetables are rich in nutrients, fiber, and antioxidants. Load up your plate with a colorful variety:

- All leafy greens
- Artichokes
- Asparagus
- Bamboo shoots
- Bean sprouts
- Beans (green or yellow wax)
- Beets
- Bok choy
- Broccoli
- Broccolini
- Brussels sprouts
- Cabbage (all varieties)
- Carrots
- Cauliflower
- Celery
- Cucumbers
- Eggplant
- Endive
- Kimchi
- Kohlrabi
- Jicama
- Mushrooms
- Okra
- Onions
- Parsley
- Peppers (all varieties and colors)
- Pickles
- Radishes
- Rutabaga
- Sauerkraut
- Scallions
- Summer squash
- Tomatoes
- Watercress
- Zucchini

Approved Starchy Vegetables:

In moderation, these starchy vegetables offer valuable nutrients and healthy carbohydrates:

- Edamame (soybeans)
- Legumes (including lentils)
- Parsnips
- Peas
- Plantains
- Potatoes
- Turnips
- Succotash (corn and lima beans)
- Sweet potatoes (yams)
- Winter squash

Approved Whole Grains:

Whole grains are a great source of fiber, vitamins, and minerals. Enjoy them in moderation for balanced carbohydrate intake:

- Amaranth (cooked similarly to rice or used as flour)
- Barley
- Brown rice
- Buckwheat (usually processed into groats, flour, or noodles)
- Bulgur
- Corn
- Farro
- Millet
- Oats
- Quinoa
- Spelt (as cooked berries or flakes)
- Wheat berries

Approved Fruits:

Packed with vitamins and antioxidants, fruits are a sweet treat you can enjoy in moderation. Stick to lower-sugar options and keep portions in check:

- Apples
- Bananas
- Blackberries
- Blueberries
- Cherries
- Cranberries (fresh)
- Grapefruit and other citrus fruits
- Pears
- Plums
- Raspberries
- Strawberries

Sugar Alternatives:

Refined sugars and artificial sweeteners are off-limits, but you can use these alternatives that don't spike insulin or glucose levels:

- Stevia and erythritol (with or without monk fruit)

Importance of Anti-Inflammatory Foods

Anti-inflammatory foods are a major focus of the Galveston Diet, and for good reason. Chronic inflammation is linked to a host of health problems, including weight gain, fatigue, and an increased risk of chronic diseases. By incorporating anti-inflammatory foods into your diet, you're helping to manage and reduce inflammation, which can lead to better overall health and well-being.

How Anti-Inflammatory Foods Help:

- Reduce Chronic Inflammation: Many of the foods emphasized in the Galveston Diet, such as fatty fish, nuts, and leafy greens, contain compounds that help reduce inflammation in the body. This can help alleviate symptoms of chronic inflammatory conditions and support overall health.

- Support Hormonal Balance: Hormones play a crucial role in regulating many of our body's functions. Anti-inflammatory foods can help maintain hormonal balance, which is especially important during menopause and midlife.

- Improve Metabolism: By reducing inflammation, these foods can help improve metabolic function, making it easier to manage weight and maintain energy levels throughout the day.

Incorporating these anti-inflammatory foods into your diet is like giving your body a daily dose of self-care. They not only help in managing weight but also support overall health by addressing the root causes of inflammation. So, load up your plate with these nutrient-packed options, and enjoy the benefits of a well-balanced, inflammation-fighting diet!

THE GALVESTON DIET LIFESTYLE

By now, you're probably getting a good feel for what the Galveston Diet is all about. You're now well-acquainted with the principles of the Galveston Diet and what to eat (and what to avoid). But there's more to this journey than just what's on your plate. Let's break down how to make the most of this diet and embrace a lifestyle that supports your goals.

Incorporating Exercise with Your Diet

We all know that diet and exercise go hand in hand when it comes to living a healthy life. Here's the thing—exercise doesn't have to be a chore, and it definitely doesn't have to mean spending hours in the gym. Here are some tips for integrating exercise into your Galveston Diet lifestyle:

1. **Find What You Enjoy:** The best exercise is the one you actually enjoy doing. Whether it's dancing, hiking, swimming, or a good old-fashioned gym workout, choose activities that make you happy. The key is consistency, and it's easier to stick with a routine if you look forward to it.

2. **Balance Your Workouts:** A well-rounded exercise routine includes a mix of cardio, strength training, and flexibility exercises. Cardio gets your heart pumping, strength training builds muscle, and flexibility exercises keep you limber. Aim for at least 150 minutes of moderate-intensity cardio per week and two days of strength training.

3. **Exercise Around Your Fasting Schedule:** Since the Galveston Diet includes intermittent fasting, consider timing your workouts to align with your eating window. Many people find it effective to exercise shortly before or after a meal. Listen to your body and see what works best for you. If you're working out in a fasted state, start with lower-intensity exercises and gradually increase as your body adjusts.

4. **Stay Active Throughout the Day:** Incorporate movement into your daily routine. Take the stairs, go for a walk during lunch, or do a quick workout at home. Every bit of activity adds up and helps you stay on track. I remember when I first started my health journey, finding time for exercise seemed impossible. But then, I discovered that integrating small, manageable workouts into my daily routine made a huge difference. For instance, I began with brisk walks in the morning before the heat kicked in. Just 30 minutes a day made me feel more energetic and balanced.

Tips for Staying Motivated

Let's face it: sticking to a new diet and lifestyle change can be challenging. I totally get it—there were days when I felt like my motivation was hiding under a rock. But don't worry, I've got some strategies to keep you motivated and committed.

1. **Set Realistic Goals:** Start by setting small, achievable goals. Instead of saying, "I'm going to lose 20 pounds in a month," aim for something more manageable, like, "I'm going to eat three servings of vegetables every day this week." Achieving these smaller goals will give you a sense of accomplishment and keep you motivated to keep going.

2. **Track Your Progress:** Whether it's through a journal, an app, or even a simple checklist on your fridge, tracking your progress can be incredibly motivating. Seeing how far you've come—whether it's weight loss, increased energy levels, or just sticking to the plan—will give you the boost you need to keep going.

3. **Reward Yourself:** Don't forget to celebrate your successes along the way! Whether it's a new workout outfit, a massage, or a fun day out, rewards can be a great way to stay motivated. Just make sure your rewards are in line with your goals (so maybe skip the donut party).

4. **Stay Connected:** Having a support system can make all the difference. Whether it's a friend, a family member, or an online community, sharing your journey with others can help keep you accountable and motivated. Plus, it's nice to know you're not in this alone!

Common Challenges and How to Overcome Them

No matter how motivated you are, challenges are inevitable. The good news? They're also totally conquerable! Here are some common obstacles and how to overcome them:

1. **Social Situations:** Eating out or attending social events can be tricky when you're trying to stick to a diet. The key is planning ahead. Look at menus beforehand, eat a healthy snack before you go, or bring a dish you know you can enjoy. Personally, I often bring a healthy dish to potlucks, so I know there's at least one option I can enjoy without straying from my goals.

2. **Cravings:** We all get cravings—especially for those foods we're trying to cut back on. When a craving hits, try to distract yourself with a walk, a glass of water, or a healthy snack. Often, cravings are more about habits than actual hunger.

3. **Time Constraints:** Busy schedules can make it hard to prepare healthy meals and exercise. Try meal prepping on weekends, choosing quick, nutritious recipes, and fitting in short bursts of activity throughout your day.

4. **Plateaus:** It's normal to hit a plateau where your progress slows down. Don't get discouraged! Mix up your routine—try new recipes, increase your exercise intensity, or add more variety to your meals.

5. **Feeling Overwhelmed:** If you ever feel overwhelmed, remember that it's okay to take things one step at a time. Focus on one aspect of the diet or lifestyle at a time, and don't be too hard on yourself if things don't go perfectly. Progress, not perfection, is the goal.

By incorporating exercise, staying motivated, and knowing how to handle challenges, you'll find that the Galveston Diet isn't just a diet—it's a lifestyle that empowers you to feel your best and live your best life.

With the foundational knowledge of the Galveston Diet and the lifestyle tips under your belt, it's time to get cooking! The next chapter is where the magic happens—where theory meets practice and your kitchen transforms into a haven of tasty, healthful meals.

CHAPTER

2

BREAKFAST ENERGIZERS

RICH IN PROTEIN

SPINACH AND FETA STUFFED OMELET

PER SERVING: CALORIES: 231KCAL | FAT: 19G | CARBS: 2G | PROTEIN: 15G

★★☆☆☆
DIFFICULTY

PREPARATION
5 minutes

COOKING
10 minutes

SERVINGS
2

INGREDIENTS

- 4 large eggs
- 1/4 cup crumbled feta cheese
- 1 cup fresh spinach, chopped
- 1 tbsp. olive oil
- Salt and pepper, to taste

DIRECTIONS

1. In your bowl, whisk the eggs with a pinch of salt and pepper.
2. Heat olive oil in a non-stick skillet over medium heat.
3. Add the spinach and sauté until wilted, about 2 minutes.
4. Pour the beaten eggs over the spinach, then cook for 3-4 minutes until the eggs are set.
5. Sprinkle feta cheese over 1/2 of the omelet, fold the other half over, then cook for another minute, until the cheese starts to melt.
6. Serve hot.

TURKEY BACON AND VEGETABLE BREAKFAST WRAP

PER SERVING: CALORIES: 292KCAL | FAT: 21.5G | CARBS: 4G | PROTEIN: 20G

★★☆☆☆
DIFFICULTY

PREPARATION
5 minutes

COOKING
10 minutes

SERVINGS
2

INGREDIENTS

- 4 slices turkey bacon
- 4 large eggs
- 1/2 cup diced bell peppers
- 1/4 cup diced onions
- 2 tbsps. olive oil
- 2 low-carb tortillas
- Salt and pepper, to taste

DIRECTIONS

1. Cook turkey bacon in a skillet over medium heat until crispy, then set aside.
2. In the same skillet, place olive oil, then sauté bell peppers and onions for 3 minutes.
3. In your bowl, beat the eggs with salt and pepper, then pour into the skillet. Scramble the eggs with the vegetables until fully cooked.
4. Place scrambled eggs and vegetables on each tortilla, add 2 slices of turkey bacon, and roll up the wrap.
5. Serve immediately.

CHICKEN AND AVOCADO BREAKFAST SALAD

PER SERVING: CALORIES: 350KCAL | FAT: 27G | CARBS: 7G | PROTEIN: 22G

DIFFICULTY

PREPARATION
10 minutes

COOKING
10 minutes

SERVINGS
2

INGREDIENTS

- 1 cup cooked chicken breast, diced
- 1 avocado, diced
- 2 cups mixed greens (spinach, arugula, kale)
- 1/4 cup cherry tomatoes, halved
- 2 tbsps. olive oil
- 1 tbsp. lemon juice
- Salt and pepper, to taste

DIRECTIONS

1. In a large bowl, combine mixed greens, cooked chicken, avocado, and cherry tomatoes.
2. In a small bowl, whisk together olive oil, lemon juice, salt, and pepper.
3. Pour the dressing over the salad and toss gently to combine.
4. Divide between two bowls and serve immediately.

SAUSAGE AND BELL PEPPER SCRAMBLE

PER SERVING: CALORIES: 310KCAL | FAT: 24G | CARBS: 4G | PROTEIN: 18G

DIFFICULTY

PREPARATION
5 minutes

COOKING
10 minutes

SERVINGS
2

INGREDIENTS

- 4 large eggs
- 2 sausages (nitrate-free), sliced
- 1/2 cup bell peppers, diced
- 1/4 cup onions, diced
- 1 tbsp. olive oil
- Salt and pepper, to taste

DIRECTIONS

1. Heat olive oil in a skillet over medium heat. Add sausage slices and cook until browned.
2. Add bell peppers and onions, sauté for 3-4 minutes until vegetables are tender.
3. In a bowl, whisk the eggs with salt and pepper, then pour into the skillet.
4. Stir gently until the eggs are fully cooked. Serve hot.

CHEESY EGG AND HAM BAKE

PER SERVING: CALORIES: 380KCAL | FAT: 30G | CARBS: 3G | PROTEIN: 22G

DIFFICULTY

PREPARATION
10 minutes

COOKING
20 minutes

SERVINGS
2

INGREDIENTS

- 4 large eggs
- 1/2 cup diced ham (nitrate-free)
- 1/2 cup shredded cheddar cheese
- 1/4 cup heavy cream
- 1 tbsp. olive oil
- Salt and pepper, to taste

DIRECTIONS

1. Preheat the oven to 375°F. Grease a small baking dish using olive oil.
2. In a bowl, whisk together eggs, heavy cream, salt, and pepper.
3. Layer diced ham in the baking dish, pour the egg mixture over it, and top with shredded cheese.
4. Bake for 20 minutes, or until the eggs are set and the cheese is bubbly.
5. Let cool slightly before serving.

SHRIMP AND SPINACH EGG MUFFINS

PER SERVING: CALORIES: 220KCAL | FAT: 15G | CARBS: 2G | PROTEIN: 18G

DIFFICULTY

PREPARATION
10 minutes

COOKING
20 minutes

SERVINGS
2

INGREDIENTS

- 6 large eggs
- 1/2 cup cooked shrimp, chopped
- 1 cup fresh spinach, chopped
- 1/4 cup diced onions
- 1/4 cup shredded cheddar cheese
- 1 tbsp. olive oil
- Salt and pepper, to taste

DIRECTIONS

1. Preheat oven to 350°F, then grease 4 muffin tin cups with olive oil (liners are not necessary but can be used for easier cleanup).
2. In a skillet, sauté onions and spinach until the spinach is wilted. Set aside.
3. In a bowl, whisk eggs, salt, and pepper. Stir in cooked shrimp, sautéed spinach, and cheddar cheese.
4. Spoon the mixture evenly into the 4 greased muffin tin cups, filling each cup about three-quarters full.
5. Bake for 18-20 minutes, or until the egg muffins are set and lightly browned on top.
6. Allow to cool slightly before serving.

STEAK AND EGG BREAKFAST BOWL

PER SERVING: CALORIES: 369KCAL | FAT: 26G | CARBS: 4G | PROTEIN: 29G

DIFFICULTY

PREPARATION
10 minutes

COOKING
15 minutes

SERVINGS
2

INGREDIENTS

- 8 oz. steak (lean cut), thinly sliced
- 4 large eggs
- 1/2 cup diced bell peppers
- 1/2 cup cherry tomatoes, halved
- 1 tbsp. olive oil
- 1 tbsp. butter
- Salt and pepper, to taste

DIRECTIONS

1. Heat olive oil in a skillet over medium-high heat. Add steak slices and cook for 3-4 minutes until browned. Season using salt and pepper, then set aside.
2. In the same skillet, add butter and sauté bell peppers until tender.
3. Whisk eggs and pour into the skillet, scrambling until cooked through.
4. Assemble the bowls by adding the scrambled eggs, steak slices, and cherry tomatoes.
5. Serve immediately.

SMOKED SALMON AND CREAM CHEESE SCRAMBLE

PER SERVING: CALORIES: 300KCAL | FAT: 23G | CARBS: 2G | PROTEIN: 19G

DIFFICULTY

PREPARATION
5 minutes

COOKING
10 minutes

SERVINGS
2

INGREDIENTS

- 4 large eggs
- 2 oz. smoked salmon, chopped
- 2 tbsp. cream cheese
- 1 tbsp. olive oil
- 1 tbsp. fresh dill, chopped
- Salt and pepper, to taste

DIRECTIONS

1. In a bowl, whisk the eggs with salt and pepper.
2. Heat olive oil in a skillet over medium heat. Add eggs and cook, stirring gently.
3. Once the eggs begin to set, add smoked salmon and cream cheese. Stir until the cheese is melted and the salmon is warmed through.
4. Sprinkle with fresh dill and serve immediately.

Chorizo and Egg Breakfast Skillet

PER SERVING: CALORIES: 330KCAL | FAT: 25G | CARBS: 4G | PROTEIN: 18G

| DIFFICULTY | PREPARATION 5 minutes | COOKING 15 minutes | SERVINGS 2 |

INGREDIENTS

- 4 oz. chorizo sausage, diced
- 4 large eggs
- 1/2 cup diced tomatoes
- 1/4 cup diced onions
- 1 tbsp. olive oil
- 1/4 cup shredded cheddar cheese
- Salt and pepper, to taste

DIRECTIONS

1. Heat olive oil in a skillet over medium heat. Add chorizo and cook until browned, about 5 minutes.
2. Add onions and tomatoes, cooking until softened.
3. In a bowl, whisk eggs with salt and pepper, then pour into the skillet. Stir gently until eggs are fully cooked.
4. Sprinkle with cheddar cheese and cook until melted.
5. Serve hot.

NOTES

ANTI-INFLAMMATORY BREAKFAST BOWLS AND SMOOTHIES

TURMERIC AND GINGER SMOOTHIE BOWL

PER SERVING: CALORIES: 310KCAL | FAT: 16G | CARBS: 38G | PROTEIN: 8G

DIFFICULTY

PREPARATION
5 minutes

COOKING
0 minutes

SERVINGS
2

INGREDIENTS

- 1 cup unsweetened almond milk
- 1 banana
- 1/2 cup frozen blueberries
- 1/2 tsp. turmeric powder
- 1/2 tsp. grated fresh ginger
- 1 tbsp. chia seeds
- 1 tbsp. almond butter
- Optional toppings: sliced banana, blueberries, chia seeds

DIRECTIONS

1. In a blender, combine almond milk, banana, frozen blueberries, turmeric powder, and grated ginger. Blend until smooth.
2. Pour the smoothie into bowls.
3. Top with a tbsp. of almond butter and optional toppings, like sliced banana, blueberries, and extra chia seeds.

AVOCADO, KALE, AND CHIA SEED BREAKFAST BOWL

PER SERVING: CALORIES: 330KCAL | FAT: 27G | CARBS: 20G | PROTEIN: 7G

DIFFICULTY

PREPARATION
10 minutes

COOKING
0 minutes

SERVINGS
2

INGREDIENTS

- 1 avocado, diced
- 1 cup chopped kale
- 2 tbsps. chia seeds
- 1/4 cup chopped nuts (almonds or walnuts)
- 1 tbsp. olive oil
- Juice of 1/2 lemon
- Salt and pepper to taste

DIRECTIONS

1. In your bowl, combine diced avocado, chopped kale, and chia seeds.
2. Drizzle with olive oil and lemon juice. Toss to mix well.
3. Top with chopped nuts and season with salt and pepper.
4. Serve immediately.

BLUEBERRY ALMOND BUTTER SMOOTHIE

PER SERVING: CALORIES: 296KCAL | FAT: 18G | CARBS: 23G | PROTEIN: 8G

DIFFICULTY **PREPARATION** **COOKING** **SERVINGS**
5 minutes 0 minutes 2

INGREDIENTS

- 1 cup unsweetened almond milk
- 1/2 cup frozen blueberries
- 2 tbsps. almond butter
- 1 tbsp. chia seeds
- 1/2 tsp. vanilla extract (optional)

DIRECTIONS

1. Blend almond milk, frozen blueberries, almond butter, and chia seeds until smooth.
2. Pour into glasses and enjoy immediately.

COCONUT MILK AND MATCHA GREEN SMOOTHIE

PER SERVING: CALORIES: 296KCAL | FAT: 23G | CARBS: 17G | PROTEIN: 6G

DIFFICULTY **PREPARATION** **COOKING** **SERVINGS**
5 minutes 10 minutes 2

INGREDIENTS

- 1 cup full-fat coconut milk
- 1/2 tsp. matcha green tea powder
- 1/2 cup frozen strawberries
- 1 tbsp. chia seeds
- 1 tbsp. almond butter

DIRECTIONS

1. Blend coconut milk, matcha powder, frozen strawberries, chia seeds, and almond butter until smooth.
2. Pour into glasses and serve immediately.

ANTI-INFLAMMATORY BERRY BREAKFAST BOWL

PER SERVING: CALORIES: 320KCAL | FAT: 19G | CARBS: 39G | PROTEIN: 10G

DIFFICULTY

PREPARATION
10 minutes

COOKING
0 minutes

SERVINGS
2

INGREDIENTS

- 1/2 cup fresh raspberries
- 1/2 cup fresh strawberries, sliced
- 1/2 cup plain full-fat Greek yogurt
- 1 tbsp. chia seeds
- 1 tbsp. almond butter
- 1 tbsp. coconut flakes (unsweetened)

DIRECTIONS

1. In a bowl, combine raspberries, sliced strawberries, and Greek yogurt.
2. Top with chia seeds, almond butter, and coconut flakes.
3. Serve immediately.

CUCUMBER AND MINT DETOX SMOOTHIE

PER SERVING: CALORIES: 58KCAL | FAT: 3G | CARBS: 6G | PROTEIN: 2G

DIFFICULTY

PREPARATION
5 minutes

COOKING
0 minutes

SERVINGS
2

INGREDIENTS

- 1 cup unsweetened almond milk
- 1/2 cucumber, peeled and chopped
- 1/4 cup fresh mint leaves
- 1 tbsp. chia seeds
- Juice of 1/2 lemon

DIRECTIONS

1. Blend almond milk, cucumber, mint leaves, chia seeds, and lemon juice until smooth.
2. Pour into glasses and serve immediately.

SPINACH AND PINEAPPLE SMOOTHIE WITH FLAXSEED

PER SERVING: CALORIES: 266KCAL | FAT: 14G | CARBS: 30G | PROTEIN: 6G

DIFFICULTY

PREPARATION
5 minutes

COOKING
0 minutes

SERVINGS
2

INGREDIENTS

- 1 cup unsweetened almond milk
- 1 cup fresh spinach
- 1/2 cup frozen pineapple chunks
- 1 tbsp. ground flaxseed
- 1 tbsp. almond butter

DIRECTIONS

1. Blend almond milk, spinach, frozen pineapple, ground flaxseed, and almond butter until smooth.
2. Pour into glasses and serve immediately.

ALMOND MILK GOLDEN TURMERIC SMOOTHIE

PER SERVING: CALORIES: 262KCAL | FAT: 15G | CARBS: 24G | PROTEIN: 8G

DIFFICULTY

PREPARATION
5 minutes

COOKING
0 minutes

SERVINGS
2

INGREDIENTS

- 1 cup unsweetened almond milk
- 1/2 tsp. turmeric powder
- 1/2 banana
- 1 tbsp. almond butter
- 1 tbsp. chia seeds
- 1/2 tsp. vanilla extract (optional)

DIRECTIONS

1. Blend almond milk, turmeric powder, banana, almond butter, chia seeds, and vanilla extract (if using) until smooth.
2. Pour into glasses and serve immediately.

QUICK BREAKFAST

SCRAMBLED EGGS WITH AVOCADO AND SALSA

PER SERVING: CALORIES: 341KCAL | FAT: 25G | CARBS: 20G | PROTEIN: 22G

DIFFICULTY

PREPARATION
5 minutes

COOKING
5 minutes

SERVINGS
2

INGREDIENTS

- 4 large eggs
- 1 avocado, diced
- 1/2 cup salsa (fresh and no added sugars)
- 1 tbsp. olive oil
- Salt and pepper to taste

DIRECTIONS

1. Heat olive oil in a skillet over medium heat.
2. Whisk the eggs in a bowl, then pour into the skillet.
3. Cook, stirring occasionally, until eggs are scrambled and cooked through.
4. Remove from heat, then stir in the diced avocado.
5. Serve with salsa on top. Season with salt and pepper to taste.

ALMOND FLOUR PANCAKES WITH BERRIES

PER SERVING: CALORIES: 296KCAL | FAT: 22G | CARBS: 13G | PROTEIN: 12G

DIFFICULTY

PREPARATION
10 minutes

COOKING
10 minutes

SERVINGS
2

INGREDIENTS

- 1 cup almond flour
- 2 large eggs
- 1/4 cup unsweetened almond milk
- 1/2 cup fresh berries (blueberries, strawberries, or raspberries)
- 1 tbsp. coconut oil

DIRECTIONS

1. In a bowl, mix almond flour, eggs, and almond milk until smooth.
2. Heat coconut oil in a skillet over medium heat.
3. Place ¼ cup of batter into the skillet for each pancake, cooking until bubbles form on the surface, then flip and cook until golden brown.
4. Serve pancakes topped with fresh berries.

COTTAGE CHEESE AND FRESH PEACHES BOWL

PER SERVING: CALORIES: 272KCAL | FAT: 14G | CARBS: 22G | PROTEIN: 17G

DIFFICULTY

PREPARATION
5 minutes

COOKING
0 minutes

SERVINGS
2

INGREDIENTS

- 1 cup full-fat cottage cheese
- 1 fresh peach, sliced
- 1 tbsp. chia seeds
- 1 tbsp. almond butter (optional)
- Cinnamon to taste (optional)

DIRECTIONS

1. In a bowl, spoon cottage cheese.
2. Top with fresh peach slices and chia seeds.
3. Drizzle with almond butter, if desired, and sprinkle with cinnamon.
4. Serve immediately.

HARD-BOILED EGGS WITH SLICED AVOCADO

PER SERVING: CALORIES: 312KCAL | FAT: 27G | CARBS: 7G | PROTEIN: 23G

DIFFICULTY

PREPARATION
10 minutes

COOKING
10 minutes

SERVINGS
2

INGREDIENTS

- 4 large eggs
- 1 avocado, sliced
- Salt and pepper to taste
- 1 tbsp. olive oil (for drizzling)
- Paprika or cayenne pepper (optional, for seasoning)

DIRECTIONS

1. Place eggs in a pot and cover with water. Bring to a boil, then reduce to a simmer for 10 minutes.
2. Remove eggs from hot water, then cool in ice water for a few minutes. Peel and slice.
3. Arrange hard-boiled egg slices on a plate with avocado slices.
4. Drizzle with olive oil, then season with salt, pepper, and optional paprika or cayenne pepper.

Quick Spinach and Cheese Breakfast Wrap

PER SERVING: CALORIES: 290KCAL | FAT: 23G | CARBS: 5G | PROTEIN: 19G

DIFFICULTY

PREPARATION
5 minutes

COOKING
5 minutes

SERVINGS
2

INGREDIENTS

- 2 large eggs
- 1 cup fresh spinach
- 1/2 cup shredded cheddar cheese
- 1 tbsp. olive oil
- Salt and pepper to taste
- 2 large tortillas or wraps (for serving)

DIRECTIONS

1. Heat olive oil in a skillet over medium heat.
2. Add in spinach and cook until wilted.
3. Whisk eggs in a bowl, then pour over the spinach.
4. Cook, stirring occasionally, until eggs are scrambled and cheese is melted.
5. Season with salt and pepper. Remove from heat.
6. Spoon the mixture onto each tortilla or wrap, then fold then roll them up to enclose the filling.

Almond Butter and Blueberry Chia Pudding

PER SERVING: CALORIES: 276KCAL | FAT: 16G | CARBS: 24G | PROTEIN: 7G

DIFFICULTY

PREPARATION
5 minutes
(plus 2 hours chilling)

COOKING
0 minutes

SERVINGS
2

INGREDIENTS

- 1 cup unsweetened almond milk
- 1/4 cup chia seeds
- 1/2 cup fresh blueberries
- 2 tbsps. almond butter
- Stevia or erythritol to taste (optional)

DIRECTIONS

1. In a bowl, combine almond milk, chia seeds, and sweetener (if using). Stir well.
2. Cover, then refrigerate for at least 2 hours or overnight, until thickened.
3. Before serving, stir in almond butter and top with fresh blueberries.

MICROWAVE SCRAMBLED EGGS WITH SPINACH

PER SERVING: CALORIES: 296KCAL | FAT: 20G | CARBS: 4G | PROTEIN: 23G

| DIFFICULTY | PREPARATION 5 minutes | COOKING 2 minutes | SERVINGS 2 |

INGREDIENTS

- 4 large eggs
- 1 cup fresh spinach
- 1 tbsp. olive oil
- Salt and pepper to taste
- 1/4 cup shredded mozzarella cheese (optional)

DIRECTIONS

1. In a microwave-safe bowl, whisk the eggs with olive oil, salt, and pepper.
2. Stir in fresh spinach.
3. Microwave on high for 1 minute, stir, then microwave for an extra 30 seconds or until eggs are set.
4. Top with shredded cheese, if desired. Serve warm.

CUCUMBER AND CREAM CHEESE ROLL-UPS

PER SERVING: CALORIES: 138KCAL | FAT: 13G | CARBS: 5G | PROTEIN: 5G

| DIFFICULTY | PREPARATION 5 minutes | COOKING 0 minutes | SERVINGS 2 |

INGREDIENTS

- 1 large cucumber
- 1/4 cup cream cheese
- 1 tbsp. fresh dill (optional)
- Salt and pepper to taste

DIRECTIONS

1. Slice cucumber lengthwise into very thin strips using a mandolin or vegetable peeler.
2. Spread a thin layer of cream cheese over each cucumber strip.
3. Sprinkle with fresh dill, salt, and pepper.
4. Roll up the cucumber strips and serve immediately.

CHAPTER

3

POWER-
PACKED
LUNCHES

SALADS WITH A TWIST

AVOCADO AND CHICKEN SALAD WITH LEMON DRESSING

PER SERVING: CALORIES: 383KCAL | FAT: 24G | CARBS: 11G | PROTEIN: 30G

DIFFICULTY

PREPARATION
10 minutes

COOKING
10 minutes
(for chicken)

SERVINGS
2

INGREDIENTS

- 1 cup cooked chicken breast, diced
- 1 avocado, diced
- 2 cups mixed salad greens (e.g., spinach, arugula)
- 1/4 cup sliced red onion
- 2 tbsps. lemon juice
- 1 tbsp. olive oil
- Salt and pepper to taste

DIRECTIONS

1. In a bowl, combine cooked chicken, avocado, salad greens, and red onion.
2. In a small bowl, whisk together olive oil, salt, lemon juice, and pepper.
3. Pour the dressing over the salad and toss to coat.
4. Serve immediately.

GREEK SALAD WITH FETA AND OLIVES

PER SERVING: CALORIES: 242KCAL | FAT: 20G | CARBS: 9G | PROTEIN: 9G

DIFFICULTY

PREPARATION
10 minutes

COOKING
0 minutes

SERVINGS
2

INGREDIENTS

- 1 cup cherry tomatoes, halved
- 1/2 cucumber, sliced
- 1/4 cup black olives, pitted
- 1/4 cup crumbled feta cheese
- 2 tbsps. olive oil
- 1 tbsp. red wine vinegar
- 1 tsp. dried oregano
- Salt and pepper to taste

DIRECTIONS

1. In a bowl, combine cherry tomatoes, cucumber, olives, and feta cheese.
2. In a small bowl, whisk together olive oil, salt, red wine vinegar, oregano, and pepper.
3. Pour the dressing over the salad and toss to coat.
4. Serve immediately.

Spinach and Bacon Salad with Avocado Vinaigrette

PER SERVING: CALORIES: 354KCAL | FAT: 30G | CARBS: 10G | PROTEIN: 15G

 **DIFFICULTY**

 PREPARATION
10 minutes

 COOKING
5 minutes
(for bacon)

 SERVINGS
2

INGREDIENTS

- 2 cups fresh spinach
- 4 strips bacon, cooked and crumbled
- 1 avocado, diced
- 1/4 cup sliced almonds
- 2 tbsps. olive oil
- 1 tbsp. apple cider vinegar
- Salt and pepper to taste

DIRECTIONS

1. In a bowl, combine spinach, crumbled bacon, avocado, and sliced almonds.
2. In a small bowl, whisk together olive oil, salt, apple cider vinegar, and pepper.
3. Pour the vinaigrette over the salad and toss to coat.
4. Serve immediately.

Roasted Beet and Goat Cheese Salad

PER SERVING: CALORIES: 328KCAL | FAT: 24G | CARBS: 18G | PROTEIN: 11G

  **DIFFICULTY**

 PREPARATION
10 minutes

 COOKING
25 minutes
(for beets)

 SERVINGS
2

INGREDIENTS

- 1 cup beets, peeled
- 2 cups mixed salad greens
- 1/4 cup crumbled goat cheese
- 1/4 cup walnuts, chopped
- 2 tbsps. olive oil
- 1 tbsp. balsamic vinegar
- Salt and pepper to taste

DIRECTIONS

1. Preheat oven to 400°F. Roast beets for 25 minutes until tender. Let cool and dice.
2. In a bowl, combine roasted beets, salad greens, goat cheese, and walnuts.
3. In a small bowl, whisk together olive oil, salt, balsamic vinegar, and pepper.
4. Pour the dressing over the salad and toss to coat.
5. Serve immediately.

MIXED GREENS WITH ALMONDS AND BERRY VINAIGRETTE

DIFFICULTY	PREPARATION	COOKING	SERVINGS
	10 minutes	0 minutes	2

INGREDIENTS

- 2 cups mixed greens
- 1/4 cup sliced almonds
- 1/4 cup fresh raspberries (or other berries)
- 2 tbsps. olive oil
- 1 tbsp. red wine vinegar
- 1 tsp. stevia or erythritol (optional for sweetness)
- Salt and pepper to taste

DIRECTIONS

1. In a bowl, combine mixed greens and sliced almonds.
2. In a blender, blend raspberries, olive oil, red wine vinegar, sweetener (if using), salt, and pepper until smooth.
3. Drizzle the berry vinaigrette over the salad and toss gently.
4. Serve immediately.

BROCCOLI AND CHEDDAR SALAD WITH CREAMY DRESSING

DIFFICULTY	PREPARATION	COOKING	SERVINGS
	10 minutes	5 minutes (for blanching broccoli)	2

INGREDIENTS

- 1 cup broccoli florets
- 1/4 cup shredded cheddar cheese
- 1/4 cup chopped walnuts
- 2 tbsps. creamy dressing (e.g., ranch or another Galveston Diet-approved version)
- Salt and pepper to taste

DIRECTIONS

1. Blanch broccoli florets in boiling water for 2-3 minutes, then cool in ice water.
2. In a bowl, combine broccoli, cheddar cheese, and walnuts.
3. Toss with creamy dressing and season with salt and pepper.
4. Serve immediately.

CUCUMBER AND TOMATO SALAD WITH HERB DRESSING

PER SERVING: CALORIES: 160KCAL | FAT: 14G | CARBS: 7G | PROTEIN: 2G

DIFFICULTY

PREPARATION
10 minutes

COOKING
0 minutes

SERVINGS
2

INGREDIENTS

- 1 cup cherry tomatoes, halved
- 1/2 cucumber, sliced (peeled if desired)
- 2 tbsps. olive oil
- 1 tbsp. red wine vinegar
- 1 tbsp. fresh herbs (e.g., parsley, basil), chopped
- Salt and pepper to taste

DIRECTIONS

1. In a bowl, combine cherry tomatoes and cucumber.
2. In a small bowl, whisk together olive oil, red wine vinegar, fresh herbs, salt, and pepper.
3. Drizzle herb dressing over the salad and toss to coat.
4. Serve immediately.

 NOTES

....

....

....

....

....

....

....

....

....

HEALTHY WRAPS AND SANDWICHES

CHICKEN AND SPINACH WRAPS WITH GARLIC AIOLI

PER SERVING: CALORIES: 265KCAL | FAT: 15G | CARBS: 8G | PROTEIN: 26G

DIFFICULTY

PREPARATION
10 minutes

COOKING
10 minutes
(for chicken)

SERVINGS
2

INGREDIENTS

- 2 large lettuce leaves
- 1 cup cooked chicken breast, shredded
- 1 cup fresh spinach
- 2 tbsps. garlic aioli (store-bought or homemade)
- 1/4 cup cherry tomatoes, halved

DIRECTIONS

1. Spread garlic aioli on the inside of each lettuce leaf.
2. Layer with shredded chicken, spinach, and cherry tomatoes.
3. Fold the sides of the lettuce to form a wrap and serve immediately.

SALMON AND CREAM CHEESE LETTUCE WRAPS

PER SERVING: CALORIES: 289KCAL | FAT: 19G | CARBS: 5G | PROTEIN: 23G

DIFFICULTY

PREPARATION
10 minutes

COOKING
0 minutes

SERVINGS
2

INGREDIENTS

- 4 large lettuce leaves (e.g., Romaine or Butter lettuce)
- 4 oz. cooked salmon, flaked
- 2 tbsps. cream cheese
- 1/4 cup diced cucumber
- 1 tbsp. fresh dill (optional)

DIRECTIONS

1. Spread cream cheese equally on the inside of each lettuce leaf.
2. Top with flaked salmon, diced cucumber, and fresh dill.
3. Fold the sides of the lettuce to form a wrap and serve immediately.

Greek Chicken Pita with Tzatziki Sauce

PER SERVING: CALORIES: 384KCAL | FAT: 14G | CARBS: 38G | PROTEIN: 27G

DIFFICULTY

PREPARATION
10 minutes

COOKING
5 minutes
(for chicken)

SERVINGS
2

INGREDIENTS

- 2 whole wheat pitas (Galveston Diet-approved, if tolerated)
- 1 cup cooked chicken breast, sliced
- 1/2 cup tzatziki sauce (store-bought or homemade)
- 1/4 cup diced cucumber
- 1/4 cup sliced Kalamata olives
- 1/4 cup crumbled feta cheese

DIRECTIONS

1. Warm the pitas in your oven or a toaster oven, if desired.
2. Spread tzatziki sauce on the inside of each pita.
3. Fill with sliced chicken, diced cucumber, Kalamata olives, and crumbled feta cheese.
4. Fold in half and serve immediately.

Beef and Vegetable Lettuce Wraps

PER SERVING: CALORIES: 293KCAL | FAT: 19G | CARBS: 10G | PROTEIN: 22G

DIFFICULTY

PREPARATION
10 minutes

COOKING
25 minutes
(for beef)

SERVINGS
2

INGREDIENTS

- 4 large lettuce leaves (e.g., Romaine or Butter lettuce)
- 1 cup lean ground beef
- ½ tsp garlic powder
- ½ tsp ground cumin
- salt and pepper, to taste
- 1/2 cup diced bell peppers
- 1/4 cup peeled and shredded carrots
- 2 tbsps. avocado oil

DIRECTIONS

1. In a skillet, heat 1 tbsp of avocado oil over medium heat. Add the ground beef and season with garlic powder, cumin, salt and pepper. Cook until fully browned and no longer pink, about 8-10 minutes.
2. In your bowl, combine cooked beef, diced bell peppers, and shredded carrots.
3. Fill each lettuce leaf using the beef mixture.
4. Drizzle the wraps with the remaining avocado oil and serve immediately.

EGG SALAD LETTUCE WRAPS WITH DILL

PER SERVING: CALORIES: 318KCAL | FAT: 25G | CARBS: 3G | PROTEIN: 21G

DIFFICULTY

PREPARATION
10 minutes

COOKING
10 minutes
(for boiling eggs)

SERVINGS
2

INGREDIENTS

- 4 large lettuce leaves (e.g., Romaine or Butter lettuce)
- 4 hard-boiled eggs, chopped
- 2 tbsps. mayonnaise (made using olive oil or avocado oil)
- 1 tbsp. fresh dill, chopped
- Salt and pepper to taste

DIRECTIONS

1. In a bowl, combine chopped eggs, mayonnaise, dill, salt, and pepper.
2. Spoon the egg salad onto each lettuce leaf.
3. Fold the sides of the lettuce to form a wrap and serve immediately.

TUNA AND AVOCADO STUFFED BELL PEPPERS

PER SERVING: CALORIES: 253KCAL | FAT: 15G | CARBS: 14G | PROTEIN: 17G

DIFFICULTY

PREPARATION
10 minutes

COOKING
0 minutes

SERVINGS
2

INGREDIENTS

- 2 large bell peppers, halved and seeded
- 1 can tuna (in water or olive oil), drained
- 1 avocado, diced
- 1/4 cup chopped red onion
- 2 tbsps. olive oil
- Salt and pepper to taste

DIRECTIONS

1. In a bowl, combine tuna, diced avocado, chopped red onion, olive oil, salt, and pepper.
2. Stuff each bell pepper half with the tuna and avocado mixture.
3. Serve immediately or chill before serving.

LIGHT AND HEARTY SOUPS

CHICKEN AND VEGETABLE SOUP WITH GINGER

PER SERVING: CALORIES: 182KCAL | FAT: 6G | CARBS: 14G | PROTEIN: 19G

★★☆☆☆

DIFFICULTY

PREPARATION
10 minutes

COOKING
25 minutes

SERVINGS
2

INGREDIENTS

- 1 cup cooked chicken breast, shredded
- 2 cups chicken broth (low sodium)
- 1 cup chopped carrots
- 1 cup chopped celery
- 1 tbsp. fresh ginger, grated
- 1/2 cup diced zucchini
- Salt and pepper to taste
- 1 tbsp. olive oil

DIRECTIONS

1. In your pot, heat olive oil over medium heat. Add carrots, celery, and ginger. Sauté for 5 minutes.
2. Add chicken broth, then bring to a boil. Reduce heat and simmer for 10 minutes.
3. Add shredded chicken and zucchini. Simmer for an additional 10 minutes.
4. Season with salt and pepper. Serve hot.

BEEF AND BROCCOLI SOUP

PER SERVING: CALORIES: 239KCAL | FAT: 14G | CARBS: 10G | PROTEIN: 21G

★★☆☆☆

DIFFICULTY

PREPARATION
10 minutes

COOKING
20 minutes

SERVINGS
2

INGREDIENTS

- 1 cup lean beef, thinly sliced
- 2 cups beef broth (low sodium)
- 1 cup chopped broccoli florets
- 1/2 cup sliced mushrooms
- 1 tbsp. olive oil
- 1 tbsp. soy sauce (or coconut aminos)
- Salt and pepper to taste

DIRECTIONS

1. In a pot, heat olive oil over medium heat. Add beef slices and cook until browned, about 5 minutes.
2. Add beef broth, then bring to a boil. Reduce heat and simmer for 10 minutes.
3. Add broccoli and mushrooms. Simmer for an additional 5 minutes.
4. Stir in soy sauce, salt, and pepper. Serve hot.

Creamy Cauliflower Soup with Chives

PER SERVING: CALORIES: 193KCAL | FAT: 14G | CARBS: 12G | PROTEIN: 5G

 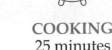

DIFFICULTY	PREPARATION	COOKING	SERVINGS
★★☆☆☆	10 minutes	25 minutes	2

INGREDIENTS

- 1 small head of cauliflower, chopped
- 2 cups vegetable broth (low sodium)
- 1/4 cup heavy cream
- 1 tbsp. olive oil
- 2 tbsps. fresh chives, chopped
- Salt and pepper to taste

DIRECTIONS

1. In a pot, heat olive oil over medium heat. Add cauliflower and cook for 5 minutes.
2. Add vegetable broth, then bring to a boil. Reduce heat, then simmer until cauliflower is tender, about 15 minutes.
3. Blend the soup until smooth (using an immersion blender or in batches using regular blender).
4. Stir in heavy cream, chives, salt, and pepper. Serve hot.

Spicy Pumpkin and Sage Soup

PER SERVING: CALORIES: 165KCAL | FAT: 7G | CARBS: 23G | PROTEIN: 2G

DIFFICULTY	PREPARATION	COOKING	SERVINGS
★★☆☆☆	10 minutes	25 minutes	2

INGREDIENTS

- 2 cups fresh pumpkin puree
- 2 cups vegetable broth (low sodium)
- 1 tbsp. olive oil
- 1 tbsp. fresh sage, chopped
- 1/2 tsp. ground cayenne pepper (adjust to taste)
- Salt and pepper to taste

DIRECTIONS

1. In a pot, heat olive oil over medium heat. Add pumpkin puree, then cook for 5 minutes.
2. Add vegetable broth, sage, cayenne pepper, salt, and pepper. Bring to a boil, then reduce heat and simmer for 15 minutes.
3. Blend the soup until smooth (using an immersion blender or in batches using regular blender). Serve hot.

ZUCCHINI AND SPINACH SOUP

PER SERVING: CALORIES: 113KCAL | FAT: 7G | CARBS: 10G | PROTEIN: 4G

DIFFICULTY   **PREPARATION**   **COOKING**   **SERVINGS**
                        10 minutes   20 minutes   2

INGREDIENTS

- 2 cups chopped zucchini
- 2 cups spinach
- 2 cups vegetable broth (low sodium)
- 1 tbsp. olive oil
- 1/2 tsp. garlic powder
- Salt and pepper to taste

DIRECTIONS

1. In a pot, heat olive oil over medium heat. Add zucchini and cook for 5 minutes.
2. Add vegetable broth and bring to a boil. Reduce heat and simmer for 10 minutes.
3. Add spinach and garlic powder. Simmer for an additional 5 minutes.
4. Blend the soup until smooth (using an immersion blender or in batches using regular blender). Serve hot.

MUSHROOM AND KALE SOUP

PER SERVING: CALORIES: 138KCAL | FAT: 7G | CARBS: 13G | PROTEIN: 6G

DIFFICULTY   **PREPARATION**   **COOKING**   **SERVINGS**
                        10 minutes   20 minutes   2

INGREDIENTS

- 1 cup sliced mushrooms
- 1 cup chopped kale
- 2 cups vegetable broth (low sodium)
- 1 tbsp. olive oil
- 1/2 tsp. thyme
- Salt and pepper to taste

DIRECTIONS

1. In a pot, heat olive oil over medium heat. Add mushrooms, then cook until soft, about 5 minutes.
2. Add vegetable broth and thyme. Bring to a boil, then reduce heat and simmer for 10 minutes.
3. Add chopped kale and simmer for an additional 5 minutes.
4. Season with salt and pepper. Serve hot.

POWER BOWLS WITH GRAINS AND GREENS

FARRO AND ROASTED VEGETABLE BOWL

PER SERVING: CALORIES: 395KCAL | FAT: 14G | CARBS: 51G | PROTEIN: 14G

DIFFICULTY

PREPARATION
15 minutes

COOKING
30 minutes

SERVINGS
2

INGREDIENTS

- 1 cup cooked farro
- 1 cup mixed vegetables (e.g., bell peppers, zucchini, and cherry tomatoes)
- 1 tbsp. olive oil
- 1 tbsp. balsamic vinegar
- 1/4 cup crumbled feta cheese
- Salt and pepper to taste

DIRECTIONS

1. Preheat oven to 400°F. Toss vegetables with salt, olive oil, and pepper. Roast for 25 minutes.
2. In a bowl, combine cooked farro with roasted vegetables.
3. Drizzle with balsamic vinegar and top with crumbled feta cheese. Serve immediately.

MILLET AND SPINACH POWER BOWL

PER SERVING: CALORIES: 305KCAL | FAT: 14G | CARBS: 34G | PROTEIN: 10G

DIFFICULTY

PREPARATION
10 minutes

COOKING
20 minutes

SERVINGS
2

INGREDIENTS

- 1 cup cooked millet
- 1 cup fresh spinach
- 1/4 cup roasted chickpeas
- 1/4 cup diced cucumber
- 1 tbsp. tahini
- 1 tbsp. lemon juice
- Salt and pepper to taste

DIRECTIONS

1. In a bowl, combine cooked millet, spinach, roasted chickpeas, and diced cucumber.
2. Drizzle with tahini and lemon juice.
3. Season with salt and pepper. Serve immediately.

BROWN RICE AND SHRIMP BOWL WITH VEGETABLES

PER SERVING: CALORIES: 351KCAL | FAT: 10G | CARBS: 38G | PROTEIN: 24G

DIFFICULTY

PREPARATION
10 minutes

COOKING
20 minutes

SERVINGS
2

INGREDIENTS

- 1 cup cooked brown rice
- 1/2 cup cooked shrimp (peeled and deveined)
- 1 tbsp. olive oil
- 1/2 cup steamed broccoli
- 1/2 cup sliced bell peppers
- 1 tbsp. soy sauce (or coconut aminos)
- Salt and pepper to taste

DIRECTIONS

1. In a skillet, heat olive oil over medium heat. Cook shrimp until pink and cooked through, for about 5 minutes.
2. In a bowl, combine cooked brown rice, steamed broccoli, and sliced bell peppers.
3. Top with cooked shrimp and drizzle with soy sauce.
4. Season with salt and pepper. Serve immediately.

BARLEY AND ROASTED CHICKEN BOWL

PER SERVING: CALORIES: 362KCAL | FAT: 10G | CARBS: 43G | PROTEIN: 23G

DIFFICULTY

PREPARATION
10 minutes

COOKING
30 minutes

SERVINGS
2

INGREDIENTS

- 1 cup cooked barley
- 1 cup roasted chicken breast, shredded
- 1/2 cup Brussels sprouts
- 1/2 cup diced carrots
- 1 tbsp. olive oil
- 1 tbsp. balsamic vinegar
- Salt and pepper to taste

DIRECTIONS

1. Preheat oven to 400°F. Toss Brussels sprouts and diced carrots with olive oil, salt, and pepper. Roast for 25 minutes.
2. In a bowl, combine cooked barley, roasted chicken, and roasted vegetables.
3. Drizzle with balsamic vinegar and mix well. Season with salt and pepper. Serve immediately.

SWEET POTATO AND BLACK BEAN POWER BOWL

PER SERVING: CALORIES: 374KCAL | FAT: 15G | CARBS: 50G | PROTEIN: 8G

DIFFICULTY

PREPARATION
15 minutes

COOKING
25 minutes

SERVINGS
2

INGREDIENTS

- 1 cup sweet potatoes (diced)
- 1/2 cup black beans (cooked or canned, rinsed)
- 1/2 cup diced avocado
- 1/4 cup chopped red onion
- 1 tbsp. olive oil
- 1 tbsp. lime juice
- Salt and pepper to taste

DIRECTIONS

1. Preheat oven to 400°F. Toss diced sweet potatoes with salt, olive oil, and pepper. Roast for 25 minutes.
2. In a bowl, combine roasted sweet potatoes, black beans, diced avocado, and chopped red onion.
3. Drizzle with lime juice and mix well. Season with salt and pepper. Serve immediately.

AMARANTH AND ROASTED RED PEPPER BOWL

PER SERVING: CALORIES: 318KCAL | FAT: 14G | CARBS: 39G | PROTEIN: 12G

DIFFICULTY

PREPARATION
10 minutes

COOKING
20 minutes

SERVINGS
2

INGREDIENTS

- 1 cup cooked amaranth
- 1/2 cup roasted red bell peppers
- 1/4 cup crumbled feta cheese
- 1/2 cup chopped spinach
- 1 tbsp. olive oil
- 1 tbsp. balsamic vinegar
- Salt and pepper to taste

DIRECTIONS

1. In your bowl, combine cooked amaranth, roasted red bell peppers, and chopped spinach.
2. Top using crumbled feta cheese and drizzle with olive oil and balsamic vinegar.
3. Season with salt and pepper. Serve immediately.

CHAPTER

4

EVENING INDULGENCES

NUTRIENT-DENSE MAIN DISHES

BAKED SALMON WITH LEMON AND DILL

PER SERVING: CALORIES: 307KCAL | FAT: 18G | CARBS: 2G | PROTEIN: 33G

DIFFICULTY

PREPARATION
10 minutes

COOKING
20 minutes

SERVINGS
2

INGREDIENTS

- 2 salmon fillets
- 1 lemon, sliced
- 2 tbsps. fresh dill, chopped
- 1 tbsp. olive oil
- Salt and pepper to taste

DIRECTIONS

1. Preheat oven to 375°F. Line a baking sheet with parchment paper.
2. Place salmon fillets on your prepared baking sheet. Drizzle with olive oil.
3. Top with lemon slices and chopped dill. Season with salt and pepper.
4. Bake for 15-20 minutes, or until salmon is cooked through, and flakes easily using a fork.

GRILLED TUNA STEAKS WITH AVOCADO SALSA

PER SERVING: CALORIES: 307KCAL | FAT: 20G | CARBS: 7G | PROTEIN: 27G

DIFFICULTY

PREPARATION
10 minutes

COOKING
0 minutes

SERVINGS
2

INGREDIENTS

- 2 tuna steaks
- 1 avocado, diced
- 1/2 cup diced tomatoes
- 1/4 cup red onion, finely chopped
- 1 tbsp. lime juice
- 1 tbsp. olive oil
- Salt and pepper to taste

DIRECTIONS

1. Preheat grill to medium-high heat. Season tuna steaks with salt and pepper on both sides.
2. Grill tuna steaks 4-5 minutes per side, or until desired doneness.
3. In a bowl, combine avocado, tomatoes, red onion, lime juice, and olive oil. Mix well.
4. Serve tuna steaks topped with avocado salsa.

SPICY SHRIMP SKEWERS WITH LIME

PER SERVING: CALORIES: 211KCAL | FAT: 8G | CARBS: 1G | PROTEIN: 31G

DIFFICULTY

PREPARATION
15 minutes
(plus, marinating time)

COOKING
10 minutes

SERVINGS
2

INGREDIENTS

- 12 large shrimp, peeled and deveined
- 1 tbsp. olive oil
- 1 tbsp. chili powder
- 1/2 tsp. cayenne pepper
- 1 clove garlic, minced
- 1 lime, juiced
- Salt to taste

DIRECTIONS

1. In a bowl, combine olive oil, chili powder, cayenne pepper, garlic, lime juice, and salt.
2. Add shrimp and marinate for at least 15 minutes.
3. Preheat grill to medium-high heat. Thread shrimp onto skewers.
4. Grill for 2-3 minutes per side, or until shrimp are pink and cooked through.

COCONUT-CRUSTED FISH WITH FRESH HERBS

PER SERVING: CALORIES: 328KCAL | FAT: 22G | CARBS: 8G | PROTEIN: 26G

DIFFICULTY

PREPARATION
10 minutes

COOKING
15 minutes

SERVINGS
2

INGREDIENTS

- 2 white fish fillets (e.g., cod or tilapia)
- 1/2 cup shredded unsweetened coconut
- 1/4 cup almond flour
- 1 egg, beaten
- 2 tbsps. coconut oil
- 2 tbsps. fresh basil, chopped
- Salt and pepper to taste

DIRECTIONS

1. Preheat oven to 375°F. Line a baking sheet with parchment paper.
2. In a bowl, mix shredded coconut and almond flour.
3. Dip fish fillets into beaten egg, then coat with coconut mixture.
4. Heat coconut oil in a skillet over medium heat. Cook fish for 2-3 minutes per side, or until golden brown.
5. Transfer fish to the baking sheet and bake for 5-7 minutes, or until fish is cooked through.
6. Garnish with chopped basil.

Herb-Roasted Chicken with Root Vegetables

PER SERVING: CALORIES: 407KCAL | FAT: 18G | CARBS: 28G | PROTEIN: 39G

DIFFICULTY

PREPARATION
15 minutes

COOKING
45 minutes

SERVINGS
2

INGREDIENTS

- 2 chicken breasts
- 1 tbsp. olive oil
- 1 tbsp. fresh rosemary, chopped
- 1 tbsp. fresh thyme, chopped
- 1 cup diced carrots, peeled
- 1 cup diced parsnips, peeled
- 1 cup diced rutabaga, peeled
- Salt and pepper to taste

DIRECTIONS

1. Preheat oven to 400°F. Line a baking dish with parchment paper.
2. Rub chicken breasts on both sides with olive oil, rosemary, thyme, salt, and pepper.
3. Place chicken in the baking dish. Surround with diced carrots, parsnips, and rutabaga.
4. Roast for 40-45 minutes, or until chicken reaches an internal temperature of 165°F and vegetables are tender.

Beef Stroganoff with Cauliflower Rice

PER SERVING: CALORIES: 383KCAL | FAT: 20G | CARBS: 15G | PROTEIN: 34G

DIFFICULTY

PREPARATION
10 minutes

COOKING
25 minutes

SERVINGS
2

INGREDIENTS

- 1/2 lb. lean beef strips
- 1 cup cauliflower rice
- 1/2 cup sliced mushrooms
- 1/4 cup full-fat sour cream
- 1 tbsp. olive oil
- 1 tbsp. Worcestershire sauce
- 1 clove garlic, minced
- Salt and pepper to taste

DIRECTIONS

1. In a skillet, heat olive oil over medium heat. Add beef strips and cook until browned.
2. Add garlic and mushrooms, cooking for an additional 5 minutes.
3. Stir in Worcestershire sauce and sour cream. Simmer for 5 minutes, or until sauce thickens.
4. In a separate pan, cook cauliflower rice according to package instructions.
5. Serve beef stroganoff over cauliflower rice.

BALSAMIC-GLAZED PORK CHOPS WITH ASPARAGUS

PER SERVING: CALORIES: 339KCAL | FAT: 19G | CARBS: 10G | PROTEIN: 31G

DIFFICULTY

PREPARATION
10 minutes

COOKING
20 minutes

SERVINGS
2

INGREDIENTS

- 2 pork chops
- 1 tbsp. olive oil
- 1/4 cup balsamic vinegar
- 1 tbsp. honey (or stevia for a low-carb option)
- 1 cup asparagus, trimmed
- Salt and pepper to taste

DIRECTIONS

1. Preheat oven to 375°F. Line a baking sheet with parchment paper.
2. Season pork chops with salt and pepper on both sides. Heat olive oil in a skillet over medium-high heat, then sear pork chops for 2-3 minutes per side.
3. Transfer pork chops to the baking sheet. Roast for 10-15 minutes, or until cooked through.
4. In a small saucepan, combine balsamic vinegar and honey. Simmer until thickened.
5. Toss asparagus with salt, olive oil, and pepper. Add to the baking sheet in a single layer, during the last 10 minutes of roasting.
6. Drizzle balsamic glaze over pork chops before serving.

STUFFED BELL PEPPERS WITH GROUND TURKEY

PER SERVING: CALORIES: 306KCAL | FAT: 13G | CARBS: 20G | PROTEIN: 25G

DIFFICULTY

PREPARATION
15 minutes

COOKING
30 minutes

SERVINGS
2

INGREDIENTS

- 2 large bell peppers
- 1/2 lb. ground turkey
- 1/2 cup cooked quinoa
- 1/2 cup diced tomatoes
- 1/4 cup chopped onion
- 1/2 tsp. garlic powder
- 1/4 cup shredded mozzarella cheese
- Salt and pepper to taste

DIRECTIONS

1. Preheat oven to 375°F. Cut the tops off the bell peppers, then remove seeds.
2. In a skillet, cook ground turkey with chopped onion, salt, and pepper until browned.
3. Stir in cooked quinoa and diced tomatoes. Mix well.
4. Stuff bell peppers with the turkey mixture and place in a baking dish, standing up.
5. Top with shredded mozzarella cheese.
6. Bake for 25-30 minutes, or until peppers are tender and cheese is melted.

Plant-Based and Vegetarian Dinner Options

Lentil and Vegetable Stir-Fry

PER SERVING: CALORIES: 307KCAL | FAT: 11G | CARBS: 39G | PROTEIN: 15G

DIFFICULTY

PREPARATION
10 minutes

COOKING
20 minutes

SERVINGS
2

INGREDIENTS

- 1 cup cooked lentils
- 1 cup bell peppers, sliced
- 1 cup broccoli florets
- 1 cup carrots, peeled and sliced
- 2 tbsps. olive oil
- 2 tbsps. soy sauce (or tamari for gluten-free)
- 1 tsp. garlic powder
- Salt and pepper to taste

DIRECTIONS

1. In a blender, combine almond milk, banana, frozen blueberries, turmeric powder, and grated ginger. Blend until smooth.
2. Pour the smoothie into bowls.
3. Top with a tbsp. of almond butter and optional toppings, like sliced banana, blueberries, and extra chia seeds.

Stuffed Eggplant with Chickpeas and Herbs

PER SERVING: CALORIES: 287KCAL | FAT: 11G | CARBS: 36G | PROTEIN: 1G

DIFFICULTY

PREPARATION
15 minutes

COOKING
30 minutes

SERVINGS
2

INGREDIENTS

- 1 large eggplant
- 1 cup cooked chickpeas
- 1/2 cup diced tomatoes
- 1/4 cup fresh parsley, chopped
- 1 tbsp. olive oil
- 1 tsp. ground cumin
- Salt and pepper to taste

DIRECTIONS

1. Preheat oven to 375°F. Cut eggplant in half lengthwise and scoop out some of the eggplant flesh to create a boat. Chop the scooped-out eggplant flesh.
2. In a bowl, mix chickpeas, diced tomatoes, chopped eggplant flesh, parsley, olive oil, cumin, salt, and pepper.
3. Stuff the eggplant halves with the chickpea mixture. Place on a baking sheet, open half facing up.
4. Bake for 25-30 minutes, or until eggplant is tender and filling is heated through.

CAULIFLOWER AND CHICKPEA CURRY

PER SERVING: CALORIES: 320KCAL | FAT: 16G | CARBS: 34G | PROTEIN: 12G

DIFFICULTY

PREPARATION
10 minutes

COOKING
20 minutes

SERVINGS
2

INGREDIENTS

- 1 cup cauliflower florets
- 1 cup cooked chickpeas
- 1/2 cup coconut milk
- 1 tbsp. curry powder
- 1 tbsp. olive oil
- 1/4 cup chopped onion
- Salt and pepper to taste

DIRECTIONS

1. Heat olive oil in a large skillet over medium heat. Add onion and cook until translucent.
2. Stir in curry powder, then cook for 1 minute.
3. Add cauliflower, chickpeas, and coconut milk. Simmer for 15-20 minutes, or until cauliflower is tender.
4. Season with salt and pepper before serving.

TEMPEH AND BROCCOLI STIR-FRY

PER SERVING: CALORIES: 306KCAL | FAT: 16G | CARBS: 23G | PROTEIN: 23G

DIFFICULTY

PREPARATION
10 minutes

COOKING
15 minutes

SERVINGS
2

INGREDIENTS

- 1 cup tempeh, cubed
- 1 cup broccoli florets
- 1 tbsp. olive oil
- 2 tbsps. soy sauce (or tamari for gluten-free)
- 1 tsp. ginger, minced
- 1 clove garlic, minced
- Salt and pepper to taste

DIRECTIONS

1. Heat olive oil in a large skillet over medium heat. Place tempeh and cook until browned, about 5 minutes.
2. Add broccoli, ginger, and garlic. Stir-fry for 5-7 minutes until broccoli is tender.
3. Stir in soy sauce, then cook for an additional 2 minutes. Season with salt and pepper.

ZUCCHINI NOODLES WITH AVOCADO PESTO

PER SERVING: CALORIES: 297KCAL | FAT: 25G | CARBS: 14G | PROTEIN: 4G

DIFFICULTY	PREPARATION	COOKING	SERVINGS
	10 minutes	5 minutes	2

INGREDIENTS

- 2 medium zucchinis, spiralized into noodles
- 1 ripe avocado
- 1/4 cup fresh basil leaves
- 2 tbsps. olive oil
- 1 clove garlic
- Salt and pepper to taste

DIRECTIONS

1. In a food processor, blend avocado, basil, olive oil, garlic, salt, and pepper until smooth.
2. In a large skillet, cook zucchini noodles over medium heat for 3-5 minutes, until slightly tender.
3. Toss zucchini noodles with avocado pesto until well-coated. Serve immediately.

SPAGHETTI SQUASH WITH TOMATO AND BASIL

PER SERVING: CALORIES: 181KCAL | FAT: 11G | CARBS: 19G | PROTEIN: 3G

DIFFICULTY	PREPARATION	COOKING	SERVINGS
	15 minutes	40 minutes	2

INGREDIENTS

- 1 medium spaghetti squash
- 1 cup cherry tomatoes, halved
- 1/4 cup fresh basil leaves, chopped
- 2 tbsps. olive oil
- 1 clove garlic, minced
- Salt and pepper to taste

DIRECTIONS

1. Preheat oven to 400°F. Cut spaghetti squash in half lengthwise, then remove seeds.
2. Drizzle the cut sides with olive oil, season using salt and pepper, and place cut-side down on a baking sheet.
3. Roast for 35-40 minutes, or until the flesh is tender and can be shredded with a fork.
4. While squash is roasting, heat olive oil in a skillet over medium heat. Add garlic and cook for 1 minute.
5. Add cherry tomatoes, then cook until softened, about 5 minutes. Stir in basil.
6. Scrape the flesh of the squash using a fork to create spaghetti-like strands. Toss with tomato mixture before serving.

MUSHROOM AND SPINACH STUFFED PORTOBELLO

PER SERVING: CALORIES: 229KCAL | FAT: 18G | CARBS: 10G | PROTEIN: 11G

DIFFICULTY

PREPARATION
10 minutes

COOKING
20 minutes

SERVINGS
2

INGREDIENTS

- 2 large portobello mushrooms
- 1 cup spinach, chopped
- 1/2 cup diced mushrooms
- 1/4 cup chopped onion
- 2 tbsps. olive oil
- 1/4 cup shredded mozzarella cheese (optional)
- Salt and pepper to taste

DIRECTIONS

1. Preheat oven to 375°F. Clean portobello mushrooms and remove stems.
2. In a skillet, heat olive oil over medium heat. Add chopped onion and diced mushrooms. Cook until softened.
3. Stir in spinach and cook until wilted. Season with salt and pepper.
4. Stuff portobello caps with the mushroom and spinach mixture. Top with mozzarella cheese if using.
5. Bake for 15-20 minutes, or until portobellos are tender.

VEGAN SHEPHERD'S PIE WITH CAULIFLOWER TOPPING

PER SERVING: CALORIES: 288KCAL | FAT: 10G | CARBS: 37G | PROTEIN: 14G

DIFFICULTY

PREPARATION
15 minutes

COOKING
30 minutes

SERVINGS
2

INGREDIENTS

- 1 cup cauliflower florets
- 1 cup cooked lentils
- 1/2 cup carrots, peeled and diced
- 1/2 cup peas
- 1/2 cup diced onions
- 2 cloves garlic, minced
- 1 tbsp. olive oil
- 1/2 cup vegetable broth
- 1 tbsp. nutritional yeast
- Salt and pepper to taste

DIRECTIONS

1. Preheat oven to 375°F.
2. Steam cauliflower florets until tender. Blend with a bit of water until smooth, to make cauliflower mash.
3. In a skillet, heat olive oil over medium heat. Add onions, carrots, and garlic. Cook until softened.
4. Stir in lentils, peas, vegetable broth, salt, and pepper. Simmer for 5 minutes.
5. Transfer lentil mixture to a baking dish and spread cauliflower mash on top.
6. Bake for 20-25 minutes, or until the top is slightly golden.

GARLIC BUTTER SHRIMP WITH ZUCCHINI

PER SERVING: CALORIES: 287KCAL | FAT: 21G | CARBS: 8G | PROTEIN: 22G

DIFFICULTY

PREPARATION
10 minutes

COOKING
10 minutes

SERVINGS
2

INGREDIENTS

- 1 lb. large shrimp, peeled and deveined
- 1 medium zucchini, sliced
- 3 tbsps. butter
- 3 cloves garlic, minced
- Salt and pepper to taste

DIRECTIONS

1. Melt butter in a large skillet over medium heat. Add garlic and cook for 1 minute.
2. Add shrimp, then cook for 2-3 minutes per side, or until pink and opaque.
3. Add zucchini and cook for extra 5 minutes, or until tender. Season with salt and pepper.

CHICKEN AND BROCCOLI STIR-FRY

PER SERVING: CALORIES: 256KCAL | FAT: 13G | CARBS: 11G | PROTEIN: 28G

DIFFICULTY

PREPARATION
10 minutes

COOKING
10 minutes

SERVINGS
2

INGREDIENTS

- 2 cups broccoli florets
- 1 lb. chicken breast, sliced into thin strips
- 2 tbsps. olive oil
- 2 tbsps. soy sauce (or tamari for gluten-free)
- 1 tsp. garlic powder

DIRECTIONS

1. Heat olive oil in a large skillet over medium-high heat. Add chicken and cook until no longer pink, about 5-7 minutes.
2. Add broccoli and garlic powder, and cook for extra 5 minutes, or until broccoli is tender-crisp.
3. Stir in soy sauce, then cook for 1 minute.

BEEF AND MUSHROOM SKILLET

PER SERVING: CALORIES: 313KCAL | FAT: 19G | CARBS: 5G | PROTEIN: 3G

DIFFICULTY

PREPARATION
10 minutes

COOKING
10 minutes

SERVINGS
2

INGREDIENTS

- 12 large shrimp, peeled and 1 lb. lean beef strips
- 1 cup mushrooms, sliced
- 2 tbsps. olive oil
- 1 tbsp. soy sauce (or tamari for gluten-free)
- Salt and pepper to taste

DIRECTIONS

1. Heat olive oil in a skillet over medium-high heat. Add beef and cook until browned, about 5 minutes.
2. Add mushrooms and soy sauce. Cook for an additional 5 minutes, or until mushrooms are tender. Season with salt and pepper.

SPICY SAUSAGE AND PEPPERS

PER SERVING: CALORIES: 370KCAL | FAT: 31G | CARBS: 10G | PROTEIN: 23G

DIFFICULTY

PREPARATION
10 minutes

COOKING
15 minutes

SERVINGS
2

INGREDIENTS

- 2 spicy Italian sausage links (nitrate-free)
- 1 red bell pepper, sliced
- 1 green bell pepper, sliced
- 1 tbsp. olive oil
- 1/2 tsp. paprika

DIRECTIONS

1. Slice sausages into bite-sized pieces.
2. Heat olive oil in a skillet over medium heat. Add sausage and cook until browned, about 5 minutes.
3. Add bell peppers and paprika, and cook for extra 10 minutes, or until peppers are tender.

TUNA SALAD WITH AVOCADO

PER SERVING: CALORIES: 297KCAL | FAT: 22G | CARBS: 8G | PROTEIN: 18G

DIFFICULTY

PREPARATION
5 minutes

COOKING
0 minutes

SERVINGS
2

INGREDIENTS

- 1 can tuna (in olive oil), drained
- 1 ripe avocado, diced
- 1/4 cup diced red onion
- 1 tbsp. lemon juice
- Salt and pepper to taste

DIRECTIONS

1. In a bowl, combine tuna, avocado, red onion, and lemon juice.
2. Season with salt and pepper. Mix gently until combined.

EGG AND SPINACH SCRAMBLE

PER SERVING: CALORIES: 213KCAL | FAT: 17G | CARBS: 2G | PROTEIN: 15G

DIFFICULTY

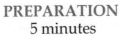

PREPARATION
5 minutes

COOKING
5 minutes

SERVINGS
2

INGREDIENTS

- 4 large eggs
- 1 cup fresh spinach
- 1 tbsp. olive oil
- Salt and pepper to taste

DIRECTIONS

1. Heat olive oil in a skillet over medium heat.
2. Add spinach and cook until wilted, about 1 minute.
3. Whisk eggs in a bowl and pour over spinach. Cook, stirring gently, until eggs are set.
4. Season with salt and pepper.

Pork Chops with Cabbage

PER SERVING: CALORIES: 324KCAL | FAT: 22G | CARBS: 8G | PROTEIN: 28G

DIFFICULTY

PREPARATION
10 minutes

COOKING
15 minutes

SERVINGS
2

INGREDIENTS

- 2 boneless pork chops
- 2 cups shredded cabbage
- 2 tbsps. olive oil
- 1 tsp. caraway seeds (optional)
- Salt and pepper to taste

DIRECTIONS

1. Heat 1 tbsp. olive oil in a skillet over medium-high heat. Season pork chops on both sides using salt and pepper, then cook for 4-5 minutes per side, until cooked through. Remove from skillet and set aside.
2. In the same skillet, place remaining olive oil and shredded cabbage. Cook, stirring occasionally, until cabbage is tender, about 10 minutes. Season with caraway seeds, salt, and pepper.
3. Serve pork chops over cabbage.

Salmon with Lemon and Herbs

PER SERVING: CALORIES: 305KCAL | FAT: 22G | CARBS: 2G | PROTEIN: 23G

DIFFICULTY

PREPARATION
10 minutes

COOKING
15 minutes

SERVINGS
2

INGREDIENTS

- 2 salmon fillets
- 2 tbsps. olive oil
- 1 lemon, sliced
- 1 tbsp. fresh dill or parsley, chopped
- Salt and pepper to taste

DIRECTIONS

1. Preheat oven to 400°F. Place salmon fillets on a baking sheet.
2. Drizzle with olive oil and season on both sides with salt and pepper. Place lemon slices on top of the fillets.
3. Bake for 12-15 minutes, or until salmon is cooked through and flakes easily using a fork.
4. Garnish using fresh dill or parsley before serving.

Turkey Meatballs with Marinara

PER SERVING: CALORIES: 295KCAL | FAT: 17G | CARBS: 6G | PROTEIN: 28G

DIFFICULTY

PREPARATION
10 minutes

COOKING
20 minutes

SERVINGS
2

INGREDIENTS

- 1 lb. ground turkey
- 1/2 cup almond flour
- 1/4 cup chopped parsley
- 1/2 cup marinara sauce (low-carb)
- 1 egg
- Salt and pepper to taste

DIRECTIONS

1. Preheat oven to 375°F. In a bowl, combine ground turkey, almond flour, parsley, egg, salt, and pepper. Mix until well combined.
2. Form mixture into meatballs, then place on a baking sheet.
3. Bake for 15-20 minutes, or until cooked through.
4. Heat marinara sauce in a skillet and serve over meatballs.

NOTES

CHAPTER

5

HEALTHY SNACK WONDERS

AVOCADO AND TOMATO SALSA WITH ALMOND CRACKERS

DIFFICULTY

PREPARATION
10 minutes

COOKING
0 minutes

SERVINGS
2

INGREDIENTS

- 1 avocado, diced
- 1 tomato, diced
- 1 tbsp. fresh cilantro, chopped
- 1 tbsp. lime juice
- 6-8 almond crackers

DIRECTIONS

1. In a bowl, combine avocado, tomato, cilantro, and lime juice. Stir gently.
2. Serve with almond crackers.

ALMOND FLOUR MUFFINS

DIFFICULTY

PREPARATION
10 minutes

COOKING
20 minutes

SERVINGS
2

INGREDIENTS

- 1 cup almond flour
- 2 large eggs
- 1/4 cup coconut oil, melted
- 2 tbsps. erythritol or stevia
- 1/2 tsp. baking powder
- 1/2 tsp. vanilla extract (optional)

DIRECTIONS

1. Preheat oven up to 350°F and line a 4-cup muffin tin with paper liners.
2. In a bowl, mix almond flour, baking powder, and sweetener.
3. In another bowl, whisk eggs, melted coconut oil, and vanilla extract.
4. Combine wet and dry ingredients, then divide the batter evenly among the 4 muffin tin cups.
5. Bake for 20 minutes or until an inserted toothpick comes out clean. Let cool before serving.

ROASTED CHICKPEAS WITH PAPRIKA

PER SERVING: CALORIES: 158KCAL | FAT: 6G | CARBS: 20G | PROTEIN: 8G

DIFFICULTY

PREPARATION
10 minutes

COOKING
30 minutes

SERVINGS
2

INGREDIENTS

- 1.5 cups cooked chickpeas
- 1 tbsp. olive oil
- 1 tsp. paprika
- 1/2 tsp. garlic powder
- Sea salt, to taste

DIRECTIONS

1. Preheat oven to 400°F.
2. Pat chickpeas dry with a paper towel.
3. Toss chickpeas with paprika, olive oil, garlic powder, and sea salt.
4. Spread on a baking sheet, then roast for 30 minutes, stirring halfway through, until crispy.

STUFFED MINI BELL PEPPERS

PER SERVING: CALORIES: 126KCAL | FAT: 10G | CARBS: 6G | PROTEIN: 4G

DIFFICULTY

PREPARATION
10 minutes

COOKING
10 minutes

SERVINGS
2

INGREDIENTS

- 8 mini bell peppers, halved and seeded
- 1/2 cup cream cheese
- 2 tbsps. fresh herbs (parsley, chives, or cilantro), chopped

DIRECTIONS

1. Preheat oven to 375°F.
2. Mix cream cheese with fresh herbs.
3. Stuff mini bell pepper halves with the cream cheese mixture.
4. Arrange on a baking sheet, then bake for 10 minutes, cream cheese side up.

BAKED KALE CHIPS

PER SERVING: CALORIES: 68KCAL | FAT: 5G | CARBS: 4G | PROTEIN: 2G

DIFFICULTY

PREPARATION
10 minutes

COOKING
15 minutes

SERVINGS
2

INGREDIENTS

- 1 bunch kale, stems removed and leaves torn into bite-sized pieces
- 1 tbsp. olive oil
- 1/2 tsp. sea salt
- 1/2 tsp. paprika (optional)

DIRECTIONS

1. Preheat oven to 350°F.
2. Toss kale leaves with olive oil, sea salt, and paprika.
3. Place on a baking sheet in a single layer.
4. Bake for 15 minutes, or until crispy, stirring halfway through.

NUT AND SEED ENERGY BALLS

PER SERVING: CALORIES: 197KCAL | FAT: 16G | CARBS: 11G | PROTEIN: 7G

DIFFICULTY

PREPARATION
10 minutes

COOKING
5 minutes
(chilling time: 30 minutes)

SERVINGS
2

INGREDIENTS

- 1/2 cup almonds
- 1/2 cup walnuts
- 1/4 cup chia seeds
- 1/4 cup sunflower seeds
- 1/4 cup unsweetened coconut flakes
- 2 tbsps. almond butter
- 1 tbsp. stevia or erythritol (optional)

DIRECTIONS

1. In a food processor, pulse almonds and walnuts until finely chopped.
2. Add chia seeds, sunflower seeds, coconut flakes, almond butter, and sweetener (if using).
3. Process until mixture holds together.
4. Form mixture into small balls, then refrigerate for at least 30 minutes before serving.

Avocado Deviled Eggs

PER SERVING: CALORIES: 220KCAL | FAT: 18G | CARBS: 8G | PROTEIN: 12G

DIFFICULTY

PREPARATION
10 minutes

COOKING
10 minutes

SERVINGS
2

INGREDIENTS

- 4 hard-boiled eggs, peeled and halved
- 1 ripe avocado
- 1 tbsp. lemon juice
- 1 tbsp. chopped chives
- Salt and pepper to taste

DIRECTIONS

1. Scoop yolks from eggs into a bowl. Mash with avocado, lemon juice, salt, and pepper.
2. Spoon or pipe the avocado mixture back into egg whites.
3. Garnish with chopped chives.

Zucchini Chips with Parmesan

PER SERVING: CALORIES: 140KCAL | FAT: 10G | CARBS: 8G | PROTEIN: 6G

DIFFICULTY

PREPARATION
10 minutes

COOKING
20 minutes

SERVINGS
2

INGREDIENTS

- 1 large zucchini, thinly sliced
- 1/4 cup grated Parmesan cheese
- 1 tbsp. olive oil
- Salt and pepper to taste
- 1/2 tsp. dried oregano

DIRECTIONS

1. Preheat oven to 400°F. Line a baking sheet with parchment paper.
2. Toss zucchini slices with salt, olive oil, pepper, and oregano.
3. Place zucchini slices in a single layer on the baking sheet.
4. Bake for 15-20 minutes, or until crispy. Sprinkle with Parmesan cheese and bake for extra 2-3 minutes.

CHERRY TOMATOES WITH MOZZARELLA BALLS

PER SERVING: CALORIES: 140KCAL | FAT: 10G | CARBS: 6G | PROTEIN: 8G

DIFFICULTY

PREPARATION
5 minutes

COOKING
0 minutes

SERVINGS
2

INGREDIENTS

- 1 cup cherry tomatoes
- 1/2 cup mozzarella balls
- 1 tbsp. olive oil
- 1 tbsp. fresh basil, chopped
- Salt and pepper to taste

DIRECTIONS

1. Arrange cherry tomatoes and mozzarella balls on a plate.
2. Drizzle with olive oil, then sprinkle with salt, basil, and pepper.

AVOCADO AND BACON BITES

PER SERVING: CALORIES: 250KCAL | FAT: 22G | CARBS: 8G | PROTEIN: 10G

DIFFICULTY

PREPARATION
10 minutes

COOKING
10 minutes

SERVINGS
2

INGREDIENTS

- 1 ripe avocado, diced
- 4 slices uncured bacon
- 1 tbsp. chopped chives
- Salt and pepper to taste

DIRECTIONS

1. Cook bacon slices in a skillet over medium heat until crispy. Drain using paper towels, then crumble into small pieces.
2. In your bowl, gently mix avocado with crumbled bacon, chives, salt, and pepper.
3. Serve immediately or chill until ready to eat.

PICKLES WITH TURKEY ROLL-UPS

PER SERVING: CALORIES: 150KCAL | FAT: 6G | CARBS: 2G | PROTEIN: 20G

DIFFICULTY

PREPARATION
5 minutes

COOKING
0 minutes

SERVINGS
2

INGREDIENTS

- 4 slices nitrate-free turkey
- 1/2 cup pickles (dill or sour)
- 1 tbsp. Dijon mustard (optional)

DIRECTIONS

1. Spread a thin layer of Dijon mustard on each turkey slice, if using.
2. Roll up each slice of turkey and secure with a toothpick, if needed.
3. Serve with pickles.

SALMON AND AVOCADO PÂTÉ WITH VEGETABLE STICKS

PER SERVING: CALORIES: 188KCAL | FAT: 13G | CARBS: 7G | PROTEIN: 12G

DIFFICULTY

PREPARATION
10 minutes

COOKING
0 minutes

SERVINGS
2

INGREDIENTS

- 1/2 cup canned salmon, drained (or cooked fresh salmon)
- 1/2 ripe avocado
- 1 tbsp. lemon juice
- 1 tbsp. chopped fresh dill
- Salt and pepper, to taste
- Vegetable sticks (e.g., cucumber, celery, bell peppers, carrots)

DIRECTIONS

1. In a bowl, mash the avocado and mix it with salmon, lemon juice, dill, salt, and pepper until well combined.
2. Serve with vegetable sticks for dipping.

CREAMY MUSHROOM AND HERB CROSTINI

PER SERVING: CALORIES: 238KCAL | FAT: 19G | CARBS: 7G | PROTEIN: 7G

DIFFICULTY

PREPARATION
10 minutes

COOKING
15 minutes

SERVINGS
2

INGREDIENTS

- 1 cup mushrooms, finely chopped
- 1 tbsp. olive oil
- 1/4 cup cream cheese
- 1 tbsp. fresh parsley, chopped
- 1 tbsp. fresh thyme, chopped
- Salt and pepper, to taste
- 4 slices low-carb bread or crackers

DIRECTIONS

1. Heat olive oil in a pan over medium heat. Add mushrooms, then cook until soft and browned, about 5-7 minutes.
2. Stir in cream cheese, parsley, thyme, salt, and pepper until well combined and creamy.
3. Toast the bread or crackers.
4. Spoon the mushroom mixture onto the toasted bread or crackers, and serve.

BUFFALO CAULIFLOWER BITES WITH BLUE CHEESE DIP

PER SERVING: CALORIES: 190KCAL | FAT: 12G | CARBS: 12G | PROTEIN: 6G

DIFFICULTY

PREPARATION
10 minutes

COOKING
20 minutes

SERVINGS
2

INGREDIENTS

- 1 head cauliflower, cut into bite-sized pieces
- 2 tbsps. buffalo sauce
- 1 tbsp. olive oil
- Salt and pepper, to taste
- For the Blue Cheese Dip:
- 1/4 cup blue cheese crumbles
- 1/4 cup Greek yogurt, full-fat
- 1 tbsp. lemon juice
- Salt and pepper, to taste

DIRECTIONS

1. Preheat oven to 400°F.
2. Toss cauliflower pieces with olive oil, buffalo sauce, salt, and pepper. Spread on a baking sheet.
3. Roast for 20 minutes, until crispy and tender.
4. For the dip: mix blue cheese crumbles, Greek yogurt, lemon juice, salt, and pepper until smooth.
5. Serve the cauliflower bites with the blue cheese dip.

STUFFED AVOCADOS WITH TUNA SALAD

PER SERVING: CALORIES: 308KCAL | FAT: 22G | CARBS: 8G | PROTEIN: 21G

DIFFICULTY

PREPARATION
10 minutes

COOKING
0 minutes

SERVINGS
2

INGREDIENTS

- 1 can tuna in water, drained
- 1/4 cup mayonnaise (preferably made with avocado oil)
- 1 tbsp. chopped celery
- 1 tbsp. chopped red onion
- 1 tsp. lemon juice
- 2 ripe avocados, halved and pitted
- Salt and pepper, to taste

DIRECTIONS

1. In a bowl, mix tuna, mayonnaise, celery, red onion, lemon juice, salt, and pepper until well combined.
2. Spoon tuna salad into the avocado halves.
3. Serve immediately or chill until ready to serve.

NOTES

 NOTES

....

....

....

....

....

....

....

....

....

....

....

....

....

....

....

....

....

CHAPTER

6

BEVERAGE BLISS

COCONUT WATER WITH LIME

PER SERVING: CALORIES: 47KCAL | FAT: 4G | CARBS: 11G | PROTEIN: 0.5G

DIFFICULTY

PREPARATION
2 minutes

COOKING
0 minutes

SERVINGS
2

INGREDIENTS

- 2 cups coconut water
- Juice of 1 lime
- Lime slices, for garnish

DIRECTIONS

1. Pour coconut water into glasses.
2. Add lime juice and stir well.
3. Garnish with lime slices and serve chilled.

AVOCADO AND SPINACH SMOOTHIE

PER SERVING: CALORIES: 156KCAL | FAT: 12G | CARBS: 9G | PROTEIN: 4G

DIFFICULTY

PREPARATION
5 minutes

COOKING
0 minutes

SERVINGS
2

INGREDIENTS

- 1/2 avocado
- 1 cup fresh spinach
- 1/2 cup unsweetened almond milk
- 1 tbsp. chia seeds
- 1/2 tbsp. stevia or erythritol (optional)

DIRECTIONS

1. Blend avocado, spinach, almond milk, chia seeds, and sweetener (if using) until smooth.
2. Pour into glasses and serve immediately.

GREEN TEA WITH MINT

PER SERVING: CALORIES: 2KCAL | FAT: 0G | CARBS: 0.6G | PROTEIN: 0G

DIFFICULTY

PREPARATION
5 minutes

COOKING
5 minutes

SERVINGS
2

INGREDIENTS

- 2 green tea bags
- 2 cups hot water
- 5-6 fresh mint leaves
- Stevia or erythritol (optional, to taste)

DIRECTIONS

1. Steep green tea bags in hot water for 5 minutes.
2. Remove tea bags and add mint leaves. Let steep for another 2 minutes.
3. Sweeten with stevia or erythritol, if desired.
4. Serve hot or chilled over ice.

ICED HERBAL TEA WITH LEMON

PER SERVING: CALORIES: 5KCAL | FAT: 0G | CARBS: 1G | PROTEIN: 0G

DIFFICULTY

PREPARATION
5 minutes

COOKING
10 minutes

SERVINGS
2

INGREDIENTS

- 2 herbal tea bags (e.g., chamomile or peppermint)
- 2 cups boiling water
- Juice of 1 lemon
- Lemon slices, for garnish

DIRECTIONS

1. Steep tea bags in boiling water for 10 minutes.
2. Remove tea bags and let cool.
3. Stir in lemon juice.
4. Chill in the refrigerator, then serve over ice with lemon slices.

CHIA SEED LEMONADE

PER SERVING: CALORIES: 21KCAL | FAT: 1G | CARBS: 3G | PROTEIN: 1G

DIFFICULTY ★☆☆☆☆

PREPARATION
5 minutes

COOKING
0 minutes

SERVINGS
2

INGREDIENTS

- 2 tbsps. chia seeds
- 2 cups water
- Juice of 2 lemons
- 1-2 tbsps. stevia or erythritol (optional, to taste)

DIRECTIONS

1. Mix chia seeds with water. then let sit for 10 minutes, stirring occasionally.
2. Stir in lemon juice and sweetener (if using).
3. Serve chilled over ice.

ALMOND MILK HOT CHOCOLATE

PER SERVING: CALORIES: 56KCAL | FAT: 3G | CARBS: 7G | PROTEIN: 1G

DIFFICULTY ★☆☆☆☆

PREPARATION
5 minutes

COOKING
5 minutes

SERVINGS
2

INGREDIENTS

- 2 cups unsweetened almond milk
- 2 tbsps. unsweetened cocoa powder
- 1-2 tbsps. stevia or erythritol (to taste)
- 1/2 tsp. vanilla extract

DIRECTIONS

1. Heat almond milk in a saucepan over medium heat until hot, but not boiling.
2. Whisk in cocoa powder and sweetener until smooth and combined.
3. Remove from heat, then stir in vanilla extract.
4. Pour into mugs and serve warm.

RASPBERRY AND COCONUT SMOOTHIE

PER SERVING: CALORIES: 142KCAL | FAT: 8G | CARBS: 14G | PROTEIN: 6G

DIFFICULTY

PREPARATION
5 minutes

COOKING
0 minutes

SERVINGS
2

INGREDIENTS

- 1/2 cup frozen raspberries
- 1/2 cup unsweetened coconut milk
- 1/2 cup Greek yogurt, full-fat
- 1 tbsp. chia seeds

DIRECTIONS

1. Blend raspberries, coconut milk, Greek yogurt, and chia seeds until smooth.
2. Pour into glasses and serve immediately.

PROTEIN-PACKED CHOCOLATE SHAKE

PER SERVING: CALORIES: 178KCAL | FAT: 11G | CARBS: 7G | PROTEIN: 15G

DIFFICULTY

PREPARATION
5 minutes

COOKING
0 minutes

SERVINGS
2

INGREDIENTS

- 1 cup unsweetened almond milk
- 1 scoop low-carb chocolate protein powder
- 1 tbsp. almond butter
- 1/2 tsp. vanilla extract
- Ice cubes (optional)

DIRECTIONS

1. Blend almond milk, protein powder, almond butter, and vanilla extract until smooth.
2. Add ice cubes if desired, then blend again.
3. Pour into glasses and serve immediately.

SPARKLING WATER WITH FRESH FRUIT

PER SERVING: CALORIES: 5KCAL | FAT: 0G | CARBS: 1G | PROTEIN: 0G

DIFFICULTY

PREPARATION
5 minutes

COOKING
0 minutes

SERVINGS
2

INGREDIENTS

- 2 cups sparkling water
- Fresh fruit slices (e.g., lemon, lime, berries)

DIRECTIONS

1. Add fresh fruit slices to glasses.
2. Pour sparkling water over the fruit.
3. Serve immediately.

SPICED HERBAL COFFEE ALTERNATIVE

PER SERVING: CALORIES: 10KCAL | FAT: 0G | CARBS: 2G | PROTEIN: 0G

DIFFICULTY

PREPARATION
5 minutes

COOKING
5 minutes

SERVINGS
2

INGREDIENTS

- 2 cups hot water
- 2 tbsps. roasted chicory root (or a similar coffee alternative)
- 1/2 tsp. cinnamon
- 1/4 tsp. nutmeg
- Stevia or erythritol (optional, to taste)

DIRECTIONS

1. Boil water and steep roasted chicory root for 5 minutes.
2. Strain and stir in cinnamon and nutmeg.
3. Sweeten with stevia or erythritol if desired.
4. Serve hot.

CHAPTER

7

28-DAYS
MEAL PLAN

If you're like me, you know that planning is half the battle when it comes to sticking to a new eating plan. That's why I've put together these comprehensive meal plans to take the guesswork out of your day and make healthy eating as effortless as possible. Over the next 28 days, you'll find a variety of delicious, nutritious meals that align perfectly with the Galveston Diet principles. Plus, I've included a vegetarian meal plan for those who like to keep it plant-powered. Each week's plan is designed to keep you satisfied, energized, and excited about your meals, with a handy shopping list to streamline your grocery trips.

WEEK 1

Day	Meal 1	Snack 1	Meal 2	Snack 2	Total Calories
1	Steak and Egg Breakfast Bowl 369kcal	Almond Flour Muffins 204kcal	Grilled Tuna Steaks with Avocado Salsa 307kcal	Avocado Deviled Eggs Avocado and Spinach Smoothie 376kcal	1256
2	Greek Chicken Pita with Tzatziki Sauce 384kcal	Buffalo Cauliflower Bites with Blue Cheese Dip 190kcal	Stuffed Eggplant with Chickpeas and Herbs 287kcal	Stuffed Avocados with Tuna Salad Coconut Water with Lime 355kcal	1216
3	Blueberry Almond Butter Smoothie Chorizo and Egg Breakfast Skillet 626kcal	Baked Kale Chips 68kcal	Chicken and Broccoli Stir-Fry 256kcal	Roasted Chickpeas with Paprika Raspberry and Coconut Smoothie 300kcal	1250
4	Egg Salad Lettuce Wraps with Dill Shrimp and Spinach Egg Muffins 538kcal	Cherry Tomatoes with Mozzarella Balls 140 kcal	Beef Stroganoff with Cauliflower Rice 383kcal	Salmon and Avocado Pâté with Veggie Sticks 188kcal	1249
5	Almond Flour Pancakes with Berries 296kcal	Stuffed Mini Bell Peppers Beef and Broccoli Soup 366kcal	Spicy Shrimp Skewers with Lime 211kcal	Nut and Seed Energy Balls Protein-Packed Chocolate Shake 375kcal	1248
6	Roasted Beet and Goat Cheese Salad 328kcal	Pickles with Turkey Roll-Ups 150 kcal	Zucchini Noodles with Avocado Pesto Beef and Mushroom Skillet 610kcal	Zucchini Chips with Parmesan 140 kcal	1228
7	Chicken and Avocado Breakfast Salad Almond Milk Golden Turmeric Smoothie 612kcal	Avocado and Tomato Salsa with Almond Crackers 181kcal	Egg and Spinach Scramble 213kcal	Creamy Mushroom and Herb Crostini 238kcal	1244

SHOPPING LIST FOR WEEK 1

PROTEINS:

- 1 lb. lean steak
- 1 lb. chicken breast
- 4 tuna steaks (about 1 lb. total)
- 12 large shrimp (about 1/2 lb.)
- 4 oz. chorizo sausage
- 4 slices nitrate-free turkey (1 small package)
- 1 can tuna in water (approx. 6 oz.)
- 1 can salmon (approx. 6 oz.) or fresh salmon fillet (1/2 lb.)
- 1 lb. lean beef strips
- 1 package cooked shrimp (about 1 cup)

EGGS AND DAIRY:

- 3 dozen large eggs
- 1 package shredded cheddar cheese (8 oz.)
- 1 small container blue cheese crumbles (4 oz.)
- 1 package cream cheese (8 oz.)
- 1 small container crumbled goat cheese (4 oz.)
- 1 container mozzarella balls (8 oz.)
- 1 small container crumbled feta cheese (4 oz.)
- 1 container Greek yogurt, full-fat (16 oz.)

FRUITS AND VEGETABLES:

- 1 bunch kale
- 1 head cauliflower
- 1 head Romaine or Butter lettuce
- 1 small bunch fresh dill
- 1 bunch fresh parsley
- 1 bunch fresh basil
- 1 bunch fresh cilantro
- 1 bunch fresh thyme
- 8 mini bell peppers
- 2 large bell peppers
- 1 large eggplant
- 1 large zucchini
- 3 avocados
- 1-pint cherry tomatoes
- 1 large tomato
- 1 package mushrooms (8 oz.)
- 1 red onion
- 1 bunch green onions
- 1 large cucumber
- 1 head broccoli or 2 cups of florets
- 1 bag mixed salad greens (5 oz.)
- 1 lime

NUTS, SEEDS, AND HEALTHY FATS:

- 1 bag almond flour (1 lb.)
- 1 bag walnuts (8 oz.)
- 1 bag almonds (8 oz.)
- 1 bag sunflower seeds (4 oz.)
- 1 bag chia seeds (8 oz.)
- 1 bag unsweetened coconut flakes (4 oz.)
- 1 jar almond butter (16 oz.)
- 1 bottle olive oil (16 oz.)
- 1 jar coconut oil (16 oz.)
- 1 jar mayonnaise (16 oz., preferably made with avocado or olive oil)
- 1 jar tzatziki sauce (12 oz.)
- 1 bottle Dijon mustard (8 oz.)
- 1 bottle soy sauce or tamari (10 oz.)
- 1 bottle Worcestershire sauce (10 oz.)
- 1 bottle balsamic vinegar (12 oz.)

GRAINS AND BREADS:

- 1 package whole wheat pitas (6 count, Galveston Diet-approved, if tolerated)
- 1 package low-carb bread (4 slices)
- 1 box almond crackers (4 oz.)

CONDIMENTS, SPICES, AND FLAVORINGS:

- 1 container salt (standard size)
- 1 container black pepper (standard size)
- 1 container garlic powder (standard size)
- 1 container paprika (standard size)
- 1 container ground cumin (standard size)
- 1 container chili powder (standard size)
- 1 jar erythritol or stevia (optional, 8 oz.)

PANTRY STAPLES:

- 1-quart unsweetened almond milk
- 1 carton beef broth (32 oz., low sodium)
- 1 bottle coconut water (16 oz.)
- 1 jar almond butter (16 oz.)
- 1 bottle buffalo sauce (12 oz.)
- 1 bottle vanilla extract (4 oz., optional)
- 1 tub low-carb chocolate protein powder (about 1 lb.)

WEEK 2

Day	Meal 1	Snack 1	Meal 2	Snack 2	Total Calories
8	Cheesy Egg and Ham Bake Chicken and Vegetable Soup with Ginger 563kcal	Avocado and Bacon Bites 250 kcal	Mushroom and Spinach Stuffed Portobello 229kcal	Roasted Chickpeas with Paprika 158kcal	1200
9	Avocado and Chicken Salad with Lemon Dressing Green Tea with Mint 385kcal	Buffalo Cauliflower Bites with Blue Cheese Dip Zucchini Chips with Parmesan 330kcal	Salmon with Lemon and Herbs 305kcal	Avocado and Tomato Salsa with Almond Crackers 181kcal	1201
10	Anti-Inflammatory Berry Breakfast Bowl Chia Seed Lemonade 341kcal	Stuffed Avocados with Tuna Salad 308kcal	Spicy Sausage and Peppers 370kcal	Nut and Seed Energy Balls 197kcal	1216
11	Chicken and Spinach Wraps with Garlic Aioli Almond Milk Hot Chocolate 322kcal	Zucchini Chips with Parmesan 196kcal	Baked Salmon with Lemon and Dill 307kcal	Stuffed Mini Bell Peppers Avocado and Bacon Bites 376kcal	1201
12	Hard-Boiled Eggs with Sliced Avocado Spiced Herbal Coffee Alternative 322kcal	Creamy Mushroom and Herb Crostini 238kcal	Lentil and Vegetable Stir-Fry 306kcal	Pickles with Turkey Roll-Ups Salmon and Avocado Pâté with Veggie Sticks 338kcal	1204
13	Tuna and Avocado Stuffed Bell Peppers Chorizo and Egg Breakfast Skillet 583kcal	Almond Flour Muffins 204kcal	Balsamic Glazed Pork Chops with Asparagus Chia Seed Lemonade 360kcal	Baked Kale Chips 68kcal	1215
14	Microwave Scrambled Eggs with Spinach 295kcal	Salmon and Avocado Pâté with Veggie Sticks 497kcal	Tuna Salad with Avocado Sausage and Bell Pepper Scramble 279kcal	Cherry Tomatoes with Mozzarella Balls 140 kcal	1211

SHOPPING LIST FOR WEEK 2

PROTEINS:

- 2 dozen large eggs
- 1 package nitrate-free ham (8 oz.)
- 1 package shredded cheddar cheese (8 oz.)
- 1 package cooked chicken breast (1 lb.)
- 2 avocados
- 1 can tuna in water or olive oil (approx. 6 oz.)
- 1 package shredded mozzarella cheese (8 oz.)
- 4 slices uncured bacon (1 small package)
- 1 package fresh or canned salmon (6 oz.)
- 1 package chorizo sausage (4 oz.)
- 1 package nitrate-free sausage links (2 links)
- 2 pork chops
- 2 salmon fillets (about 1 lb.)
- 1 package spicy sausage links (2 links)
- 4 slices nitrate-free turkey (1 small package)

DAIRY:

- 1 carton heavy cream (8 oz.)
- 1 container full-fat Greek yogurt (16 oz.)
- 1 package blue cheese crumbles (4 oz.)
- 1 package cream cheese (8 oz.)
- 1 container mozzarella balls (8 oz.)

FRUITS AND VEGETABLES:

- 1-pint fresh raspberries
- 1-pint fresh strawberries
- 1 head cauliflower
- 1 bunch kale
- 1 bag mixed salad greens (5 oz.)
- 1 large red onion
- 1 bunch fresh parsley
- 1 bunch fresh thyme
- 1 bunch fresh dill
- 1 bunch fresh cilantro
- 1 bunch fresh basil
- 1 head Romaine or Butter lettuce
- 1 large zucchini
- 8 mini bell peppers
- 2 large bell peppers
- 1-pint cherry tomatoes
- 1 large tomato
- 1 package mushrooms (8 oz.)
- 1 head broccoli or 2 cups of florets
- 1 bunch fresh mint
- 1 cucumber
- 1 bunch asparagus
- 1 bunch green onions
- 1 bunch fresh ginger
- 1 lemon
- 1 lime
- 1 bag of vegetable sticks (e.g., cucumber, celery, bell peppers)
- 1 large carrot
- 1 package spinach (8 oz.)
- 2 large portobello mushrooms
- 1 can pickles (dill or sour)

NUTS, SEEDS, AND HEALTHY FATS:

- 1 bag chia seeds (8 oz.)
- 1 jar almond butter (16 oz.)
- 1 bag unsweetened coconut flakes (4 oz.)
- 1 bag almonds (8 oz.)
- 1 bag walnuts (8 oz.)
- 1 bag sunflower seeds (4 oz.)
- 1 bag almond flour (1 lb.)

PANTRY STAPLES:

- 1 bottle olive oil (16 oz.)
- 1 bottle balsamic vinegar (12 oz.)
- 1 bottle soy sauce or tamari (10 oz.)
- 1 jar mayonnaise (16 oz, preferably made with avocado oil)
- 1 bottle Dijon mustard (8 oz.)
- 1 jar tzatziki sauce (12 oz.)
- 1 bottle buffalo sauce (12 oz.)
- 1 container salt (standard size)
- 1 container black pepper (standard size)
- 1 container paprika (standard size)
- 1 container garlic powder (standard size)
- 1 container dried oregano (standard size)
- 1 jar erythritol or stevia (optional, 8 oz.)
- 1 jar honey (8 oz., or stevia for low-carb)
- 1 bottle vanilla extract (4 oz., optional)
- 1 carton chicken broth (32 oz., low sodium)
- 1 can chickpeas (15 oz.)
- 1 package almond crackers (4 oz.)
- 1-quart unsweetened almond milk
- 1 container cocoa powder (8 oz.)

BEVERAGES AND SNACKS:

- 2 green tea bags
- 1 package roasted chicory root (8 oz.)
- 1 container stevia or erythritol (optional, 8 oz.)

WEEK 3

Day	Meal 1	Snack 1	Meal 2	Snack 2	Total Calories
15	Spinach and Feta Stuffed Omelet Beef and Broccoli Soup *470kcal*	Avocado Deviled Eggs Spiced Herbal Coffee Alternative *130kcal*	Cauliflower and Chickpea Curry *320kcal*	Avocado and Tomato Salsa with Almond Crackers *181kcal*	*1101*
16	Spinach Bacon Salad with Avocado Vinaigrette *354kcal*	Roasted Chickpeas with Paprika Avocado and Bacon Bites *408kcal*	Garlic Butter Shrimp with Zucchini *287kcal*	Pickles with Turkey Roll-Ups *150kcal*	*1199*
17	Spinach and Pineapple Smoothie with Flaxseed Barley and Roasted Chicken Bowl *628kcal*	Creamy Mushroom and Herb Crostini *238kcal*	Turkey Meatballs with Marinara *295kcal*	Baked Kale Chips *68kcal*	*1229*
18	Beef and Veggie Lettuce Wraps Sweet Potato and Black Bean Power Bowl *666kcal*	Buffalo Cauliflower Bites with Blue Cheese Dip *190kcal*	Spaghetti Squash with Tomato and Basil Coconut Water with Lime *227kcal*	Cherry Tomatoes with Mozzarella Balls *140kcal*	*1223*
19	Almond Butter and Blueberry Chia Pudding Raspberry and Coconut Smoothie *418kcal*	Almond Flour Muffins *204kcal*	Herb-Roasted Chicken with Root Vegetables *407kcal*	Salmon and Avocado Pâté with Veggie Sticks *188kcal*	*1217*
20	Broccoli and Cheddar Salad with Creamy Dressing Brown Rice and Shrimp Bowl with Veggies *622kcal*	Nut and Seed Energy Balls *197kcal*	Vegan Shepherd's Pie with Cauliflower Topping *288kcal*	Stuffed Mini Bell Peppers *126kcal*	*1233*
21	Smoked Salmon and Cream Cheese Scramble *300kcal*	Avocado and Bacon Bites *250kcal*	Coconut-Crusted Fish with Fresh Herbs Chicken and Broccoli Stir-Fry *585kcal*	Zucchini Chips with Parmesan *140kcal*	*1275*

SHOPPING LIST FOR WEEK 3

PROTEINS:

- 2 dozen large eggs
- 1 lb. large shrimp, peeled and deveined
- 1 lb. ground turkey
- 2 chicken breasts (about 1 lb.)
- 1 lb. lean ground beef
- 1 package nitrate-free turkey slices (4 slices)
- 4 strips bacon, uncured (1 small package)
- 2 white fish fillets (e.g., cod or tilapia)
- 1 lb. chicken breast, sliced into thin strips
- 1 small package smoked salmon (2 oz.)
- 1 can salmon (approx. 6 oz.) or fresh salmon fillet (1/2 lb.)
- 1 can black beans (15 oz., low sodium, or cooked)
- 1 package cooked shrimp (about 1 cup)
- 1 package roasted chicken breast (shredded, about 1 cup)

EGGS AND DAIRY:

- 1 small container crumbled feta cheese (4 oz.)
- 1 small container crumbled blue cheese (4 oz.)
- 1 package cream cheese (8 oz.)
- 1 container full-fat Greek yogurt (16 oz.)
- 1 container mozzarella balls (8 oz.)
- 1 small package shredded cheddar cheese (8 oz.)

FRUITS AND VEGETABLES:

- 2 bunches fresh spinach
- 1 bunch fresh chives
- 1 head cauliflower
- 1 head kale
- 1 bunch fresh cilantro
- 1 bunch fresh parsley
- 1 bunch fresh thyme
- 1 bunch fresh dill
- 1 bunch fresh basil
- 8 mini bell peppers
- 2 large bell peppers
- 1 medium zucchini
- 1 large zucchini
- 3 avocados
- 2 ripe avocados
- 1 package cherry tomatoes (1 pint)
- 1 large tomato
- 1 package mushrooms (8 oz.)

- 1 red onion
- 1 bunch green onions
- 1 head broccoli or 2 cups of florets
- 1 small bunch fresh rosemary
- 1 bunch fresh basil
- 1 large lettuce head (Romaine or Butter lettuce)
- 1 head of garlic
- 1 medium spaghetti squash
- 1 bunch fresh herbs (parsley, chives, cilantro)
- 2 medium carrots
- 1 medium parsnip
- 1 medium rutabaga
- 1 package cherry tomatoes
- 1 small bag shredded carrots (about 1 cup)
- 1 bunch fresh thyme
- 1 bunch fresh rosemary
- 1 bag mixed salad greens (5 oz.)
- 1 lime
- 1 cucumber
- 1-pint cherry tomatoes
- 1 small bag baby spinach
- 2 cups vegetable sticks (cucumber, celery, bell peppers)
- 1 small bag of shredded Brussels sprouts
- 1 lb. sweet potatoes

NUTS, SEEDS, AND HEALTHY FATS:

- 1 small bag of chia seeds (8 oz.)
- 1 bag almonds (8 oz.)
- 1 bag walnuts (8 oz.)
- 1 bag sunflower seeds (4 oz.)
- 1 bag unsweetened coconut flakes (4 oz.)
- 1 jar almond butter (16 oz.)
- 1 bottle olive oil (16 oz.)
- 1 jar coconut oil (16 oz.)
- 1 bottle avocado oil (12 oz.)

GRAINS, BREADS, AND CRACKERS:

- 1 package almond flour (1 lb.)
- 1 box almond crackers (4 oz.)
- 1 small bag brown rice (1 lb.)
- 1 package low-carb bread (4 slices)

CONDIMENTS, SPICES, AND FLAVORINGS:

- 1 bottle Dijon mustard (8 oz.)
- 1 bottle apple cider vinegar (12 oz.)
- 1 bottle soy sauce or tamari (10 oz.)
- 1 bottle balsamic vinegar (12 oz.)
- 1 bottle buffalo sauce (12 oz.)
- 1 jar nutritional yeast (4 oz.)
- 1 bottle vanilla extract (4 oz., optional)
- 1 jar erythritol or stevia (optional, 8 oz.)
- 1 small container of creamy dressing (e.g., ranch or Galveston Diet-approved version, 8 oz.)

PANTRY STAPLES:

- 1-quart unsweetened almond milk
- 1 carton beef broth (32 oz., low sodium)
- 1 bottle coconut water (16 oz.)
- 1 package roasted chicory root (8 oz., or similar coffee alternative)
- 1 can chickpeas (15 oz., or 2 cups cooked chickpeas)
- 1 can lentils (15 oz., or 1 cup cooked lentils)
- 1 jar marinara sauce (low-carb, 16 oz.)
- 1 package baking powder (standard size)
- 1 jar Dijon mustard (8 oz.)
- 1 bag shredded Parmesan cheese (4 oz.)
- 1 package coconut milk (16 oz.)

WEEK 4

Day	Meal 1	Snack 1	Meal 2	Snack 2	Total Calories
22	Turkey Bacon and Veggie Breakfast Wrap Spicy Pumpkin and Sage Soup 457kcal	Stuffed Avocados with Tuna Salad 308kcal	Beef and Mushroom Skillet 313kcal	Stuffed Mini Bell Peppers 126kcal	1204
23	Salmon and Cream Cheese Lettuce Wraps Amaranth and Roasted Pepper Bowl 606kcal	Avocado and Tomato Salsa with Almond Crackers 181kcal	Stuffed Bell Peppers with Ground Turkey 306kcal	Cherry Tomatoes with Mozzarella Balls 140kcal	1233
24	Avocado, Kale, and Chia Seed Breakfast Bowl Chicken and Vegetable Soup with Ginger 513kcal	Salmon and Avocado Pâté with Veggie Sticks 188kcal	Tempeh and Broccoli Stir-Fry 306kcal	Nut and Seed Energy Balls 197kcal	1204
25	Mushroom and Kale Soup Lentil and Vegetable Stir-Fry 444kcal	Almond Flour Muffins 204kcal	Pork Chops with Cabbage 324kcal	Avocado and Bacon Bites 250kcal	1222
26	Scrambled Eggs with Avocado and Salsa 341kcal	Avocado Deviled Eggs 220kcal	Beef Stroganoff with Cauliflower Rice 383kcal	Buffalo Cauliflower Bites with Blue Cheese Dip Zucchini Chips with Parmesan 330kcal	1274
27	Millet and Spinach Power Bowl 305kcal	Roasted Chickpeas with Paprika 158kcal	Spicy Shrimp Skewers with Lime Beef Stroganoff with Cauliflower Rice 593kcal	Zucchini Chips with Parmesan Sparkling Water with Fresh Fruit 145kcal	1201
28	Quick Spinach and Cheese Breakfast Wrap 290kcal	Creamy Mushroom and Herb Crostini 238kcal	Zucchini Noodles with Avocado Pesto Beef and Mushroom Skillet 610kcal	Baked Kale Chips 68kcal	1206

SHOPPING LIST FOR WEEK 4

PROTEINS:

- 1 package (4 slices) turkey bacon
- 1 lb. cooked salmon fillet or 1 can (6 oz.) salmon
- 1 package shredded cheddar cheese (8 oz.)
- 1 package mozzarella balls (8 oz.)
- 1 container cream cheese (8 oz.)
- 1 can tuna in water (approx. 6 oz.)
- 1 lb. ground turkey
- 1 package lean beef strips (1 lb.)
- 2 boneless pork chops
- 12 large shrimp (about 1/2 lb.)
- 1 package tempeh (8 oz.)
- 1 lb. chicken breast
- 1 package nitrate-free uncured bacon (4 slices)

EGGS AND DAIRY:

- 2 dozen large eggs
- 1 container full-fat Greek yogurt (16 oz.)
- 1 container sour cream (8 oz.)
- 1 package feta cheese (4 oz.)
- 1 package shredded mozzarella (8 oz.)
- 1 package blue cheese crumbles (4 oz.)

FRUITS AND VEGETABLES:

- 3 large avocados
- 1 head cauliflower
- 1 bunch kale
- 2 large bell peppers
- 1 small bunch fresh dill
- 1 small bunch fresh thyme
- 1 bunch parsley
- 1 head Romaine or Butter lettuce
- 1 cucumber
- 1-pint cherry tomatoes
- 1 large tomato
- 1 large zucchini
- 2 medium zucchinis (for spiralizing)
- 1 bunch green onions
- 1 head broccoli or 2 cups broccoli florets
- 1 small container fresh spinach (5 oz.)
- 1 bunch fresh cilantro
- 1 lime
- 1 lemon

- 1 red onion
- 1 package mushrooms (8 oz.)
- 1 bunch fresh sage
- 1 cup fresh pumpkin puree or 1 small pumpkin (for fresh puree)
- 2 cups shredded cabbage
- 1 small bunch fresh basil
- 1 head celery
- 1 bag mixed salad greens (5 oz.)
- 1 bag mini bell peppers (8 count)
- 1 cup sliced mushrooms

NUTS, SEEDS, AND HEALTHY FATS:

- 1 package chia seeds (8 oz.)
- 1 bag almonds (8 oz.)
- 1 bag walnuts (8 oz.)
- 1 bag sunflower seeds (4 oz.)
- 1 package unsweetened coconut flakes (4 oz.)
- 1 jar almond butter (16 oz.)
- 1 bottle olive oil (16 oz.)
- 1 jar coconut oil (16 oz.)
- 1 bottle almond flour (1 lb.)

GRAINS AND BREADS:

- 1 package low-carb tortillas (6 count)
- 1 package low-carb bread (4 slices)
- 1 box almond crackers (4 oz.)
- 1 package cooked millet (8 oz.)
- 1 package cooked quinoa (8 oz.)
- 1 package cooked amaranth (8 oz.)
- 1 package roasted chickpeas (8 oz.)

PANTRY STAPLES:

- 1 bottle soy sauce or tamari (10 oz.)
- 1 bottle Worcestershire sauce (10 oz.)
- 1 jar mayonnaise (16 oz., preferably made with avocado or olive oil)
- 1 bottle buffalo sauce (12 oz.)
- 1 bottle Dijon mustard (8 oz.)
- 1 container vegetable broth (32 oz., low sodium)
- 1 container chicken broth (32 oz., low sodium)
- 1 bottle balsamic vinegar (12 oz.)
- 1 bottle vanilla extract (4 oz., optional)

CONDIMENTS, SPICES, AND FLAVORINGS:

- 1 container sea salt (standard size)
- 1 container black pepper (standard size)
- 1 container garlic powder (standard size)
- 1 container paprika (standard size)
- 1 container dried oregano (standard size)
- 1 container ground cumin (standard size)
- 1 container chili powder (standard size)
- 1 jar stevia or erythritol (optional, 8 oz.)

BEVERAGES:

- 1 bottle sparkling water (16 oz.)
- Fresh fruit slices (lemon, lime, or berries)

Vegetarian Menus

Day	Meal 1	Snack 1	Meal 2	Snack 2	Total Calories
1	Coconut Milk and Matcha Green Smoothie 296kcal	Nut and Seed Energy Balls Protein-Packed Chocolate Shake 375kcal	Stuffed Eggplant with Chickpeas and Herbs Avocado and Spinach Smoothie 442kcal	Stuffed Mini Bell Peppers 126kcal	1239
2	Zucchini and Spinach Soup Amaranth and Roasted Pepper Bowl 440kcal	Avocado and Tomato Salsa with Almond Crackers 181kcal	Tempeh and Broccoli Stir-Fry Raspberry and Coconut Smoothie 449kcal	Roasted Chickpeas with Paprika 158kcal	1228
3	Turmeric and Ginger Smoothie Bowl Cottage Cheese and Fresh Peach Bowl 583kcal	Stuffed Mini Bell Peppers 126kcal	Lentil and Vegetable Stir-Fry 306kcal	Nut and Seed Energy Balls 197kcal	1212
4	Creamy Cauliflower Soup with Chives Protein-Packed Chocolate Shake 371kcal	Roasted Chickpeas with Paprika 158kcal	Cauliflower and Chickpea Curry Spicy Pumpkin and Sage Soup 485kcal	Avocado and Tomato Salsa with Almond Crackers Iced Herbal Tea with Lemon 186kcal	1200
5	Greek Salad with Feta and Olives Farro and Roasted Vegetable Bowl 637kcal	Nut and Seed Energy Balls 197kcal	Stuffed Eggplant with Chickpeas and Herbs 287kcal	Stuffed Mini Bell Peppers 126kcal	1247
6	Cucumber and Tomato Salad with Herb Dressing Almond Milk Golden Turmeric Smoothie 423kcal	Avocado and Tomato Salsa with Almond Crackers 181kcal	Tempeh and Broccoli Stir-Fry Cucumber and Cream Cheese Roll-Ups 445kcal	Roasted Chickpeas with Paprika 158kcal	1207
7	Mixed Greens with Almonds and Berry Vinaigrette Raspberry and Coconut Smoothie 395kcal	Stuffed Mini Bell Peppers Coconut Water with Lime 173kcal	Lentil and Vegetable Stir-Fry 306kcal	Nut and Seed Energy Balls 462kcal	1336

Shopping List for Vegetarian Menus

PROTEINS AND DAIRY::

- 1 dozen large eggs
- 1 package shredded cheddar cheese (8 oz.)
- 1 small container crumbled feta cheese (4 oz.)
- 1 small container full-fat Greek yogurt (16 oz.)
- 1 small container full-fat cottage cheese (16 oz.)
- 1 package cream cheese (8 oz.)
- 1 small container heavy cream (8 oz.)
- 1 container low-carb chocolate protein powder (about 1 lb.)

FRUITS AND VEGETABLES:

- 1 small bunch fresh spinach
- 1 head cauliflower
- 1 small head of broccoli (or 1 cup florets)
- 8 mini bell peppers
- 1 large zucchini
- 1 large eggplant
- 1 bunch fresh chives
- 1 bunch fresh parsley
- 1 bunch fresh cilantro
- 1 bunch fresh basil
- 1 bunch fresh dill
- 1 bunch fresh sage
- 1-pint cherry tomatoes
- 2 large tomatoes
- 1 large cucumber
- 1 bunch bananas (about 5-6)
- 1 fresh peach
- 1 large avocado
- 1 small bag frozen raspberries (10-12 oz.)
- 1 small bag frozen strawberries (10-12 oz.)
- 1 small bag frozen blueberries (10-12 oz.)
- 2 medium onions
- 1 large cucumber
- 1 package mixed greens (5 oz.)
- 1 small pumpkin or 1 can pumpkin puree (15 oz.)
- 1 lime
- 1 lemon
- 1 small head of cauliflower
- 2 cups coconut water (1 bottle)
- 2 cups vegetable broth (low sodium, 32 oz. carton)
- 1 package tempeh (8 oz.)
- 1 bag farro (1 lb.)

NUTS, SEEDS, AND HEALTHY FATS:

- 1 small bag chia seeds (8 oz.)
- 1 small bag almond flour (1 lb.)
- 1 small bag walnuts (8 oz.)
- 1 small bag almonds (8 oz.)
- 1 small bag sunflower seeds (4 oz.)
- 1 small bag unsweetened coconut flakes (4 oz.)
- 1 jar almond butter (16 oz.)
- 1 bottle olive oil (16 oz.)
- 1 bottle coconut oil (16 oz.)

BEVERAGES AND CONDIMENTS:

- 1 can full-fat coconut milk (13.5 oz.)
- 1-quart unsweetened almond milk
- 1 bottle soy sauce or tamari (10 oz.)
- 1 bottle red wine vinegar (8 oz.)
- 1 bottle balsamic vinegar (12 oz.)
- 1 small bottle vanilla extract (4 oz.)
- 1 small jar stevia or erythritol (optional, 8 oz.)
- 1 box herbal tea (20 bags, chamomile or peppermint)
- 1 small jar Dijon mustard (8 oz.)
- 1 bottle buffalo sauce (12 oz.)
- 1 bottle Worcestershire sauce (10 oz.)

SPICES AND FLAVORINGS:

- 1 container salt (standard size)
- 1 container black pepper (standard size)
- 1 container garlic powder (standard size)
- 1 container paprika (standard size)
- 1 container ground cumin (standard size)
- 1 container turmeric powder (standard size)
- 1 small jar matcha green tea powder (1 oz.)
- 1 container ground cayenne pepper (standard size)
- 1 container dried oregano (standard size)
- 1 small piece fresh ginger (about 4 oz.)

"The secret of getting ahead is getting started.»"

- Mark Twain -

CONCLUSION

Congratulations! You've made it to the end of The Galveston Diet Cookbook for Beginners, and I couldn't be more excited for you! I hope you're feeling empowered, inspired, and ready to make lasting changes to your health and wellness. By now, you've absorbed the core principles of the Galveston Diet and seen firsthand how it's designed specifically for women in midlife. You've learned that this journey isn't about deprivation or strict rules, but about nourishing your body, making sustainable choices, and finding joy in the process.

Recap of Key Takeaways

Let's quickly review the main ideas and takeaways we've covered in this book:

1. **The Foundations of the Galveston Diet:** The Galveston Diet was developed by Dr. Mary Claire Haver, an OB-GYN, after realizing that the standard advice of "eat less, move more" wasn't cutting it for her or many of her patients, particularly those experiencing menopause. Understanding the hormonal shifts that women go through in midlife led to the creation of a diet that focuses on intermittent fasting, anti-inflammatory foods, and macronutrient tracking. These principles were designed specifically for women to help address common midlife issues like unwanted weight gain, low energy, and inflammation.

2. **Intermittent Fasting:** One of the biggest misconceptions about intermittent fasting is that it means depriving yourself. But as we've learned, fasting is about giving your body a break from constant digestion so it can focus on healing and fat-burning. And guess what? It works. You don't have to give up the foods you love or feel like you're missing out. Fasting is flexible, and it's something you can adapt to fit your unique schedule and needs.

3. **The Power of Anti-Inflammatory Foods:** Inflammation is one of the biggest challenges women face in midlife, especially as our hormones fluctuate. Throughout this cookbook, we've focused on incorporating anti-inflammatory foods that combat this issue, like leafy greens, healthy fats, and berries. These foods don't just help reduce inflammation—they can also help improve digestion, boost your immune system, and even brighten your mood. The recipes in this book were crafted with this in mind, giving you delicious and nutritious options to fuel your body and reduce internal stress.

4. **Macronutrient Tracking:** While calorie counting can feel tedious and restrictive, macronutrient tracking is all about balance. The Galveston Diet encourages focusing on healthy fats, lean proteins, and complex carbohydrates to ensure you're getting the right nutrients in the right amounts. By paying attention to your macronutrient intake, you can support muscle growth, balance your hormones, and stay energized throughout the day.

5. **Incorporating Exercise:** We also touched on the importance of exercise in combination with the Galveston Diet. Whether it's walking, yoga, strength training, or something more intense, exercise helps support the diet's goals by boosting your metabolism, building lean muscle, and improving your overall sense of well-being. The key is finding activities you enjoy so that movement becomes a natural part of your lifestyle.

6. **Staying Motivated and Overcoming Challenges:** We all know that motivation can be hard to maintain, especially when life gets busy or stress creeps in. Throughout this book, I've shared some tips on how to stay motivated and push through the difficult moments. The most important thing to remember is that progress is progress, no matter how small. It's about the long game—building habits that support your goals day in and day out.

7. **Meal Plans and Recipes for Success:** This cookbook was designed to take the guesswork out of eating on the Galveston Diet. I've provided you with meal plans and weekly shopping lists to simplify your life, as well as plenty of tasty recipes that make healthy eating feel like less of a chore. The recipes are meant to nourish your body, satisfy your cravings, and help you build a sustainable relationship with food.

As you wrap up this book, remember that change is possible at any stage of life. Midlife doesn't have to mean slowing down or feeling out of control. The Galveston Diet is here to support you in regaining your energy, confidence, and vitality.

I know how challenging it can be to navigate this phase of life. But trust me, with the right approach, you can not only meet your goals but exceed them. Whether you're here to lose weight, boost your energy, or simply feel healthier, you're capable of achieving it.

Now that you've got all the tools and knowledge at your fingertips, it's time to take action because knowledge is only powerful when you apply it. I encourage you to start by putting your meal plan and shopping list into practice. Pick a week, dive into the recipes that excite you the most, prepare your meals, and see how you feel. Notice the changes in your energy, your mood, and how your body responds.

I can tell you from personal experience—this lifestyle doesn't happen overnight. When I first began my journey with the Galveston Diet, I made my fair share of mistakes. Some days I'd forget to fast or find myself craving foods that weren't exactly in line with the plan. But over time, as I listened to my body, embraced flexibility, and stayed committed to the principles, I found a rhythm that worked for me. And you will too!

Remember, this journey is about progress, not perfection. You don't have to get it all right from the start, and it's okay to have moments where you slip up. What matters most is that you keep going and keep making choices that honor your body and health.

If you ever feel stuck or need a little extra motivation, just revisit the recipes, tips, and strategies in this book. There's always something new to learn or a different way to approach your routine. And if you ever need a reminder of why you started, just think about how much better you feel when you nourish your body with love and care.

So, what are you waiting for? Let's put everything you've learned into action and start living the vibrant, healthy life you deserve. The next chapter of your health journey is right in front of you, and I can't wait to see where it takes you!

You've got this. Now go and make the Galveston Diet work for you!

APPENDIX: MEASUREMENT CONVERSION CHART

Volume Equivalents (Dry)	
US Standard	Metric (approximate)
1/8 teaspoon	0.5 mL
¼ teaspoon	1 mL
½ teaspoon	2 mL
¾ teaspoon	4 mL
1 teaspoon	5 mL
1 tablespoon	15 mL
¼ cup	59 mL
½ cup	118 mL
¾ cup	177 mL
1 cup	235 mL
2 cup	475 mL
3 cup	700 mL
4 cup	1 L

Volume Equivalents (Dry)		
US Standard	US Standard (Ounces)	Metric (approximate)
2 tablespoons	1 fl. oz.	30 mL
¼	2 fl. oz.	60 mL
½	4 fl. oz.	120 mL
1	8 fl. oz.	240 mL
1 ½	12 fl. oz.	355 mL
2 cups or 1 pint	16 fl. oz.	475 mL
4 cups or 1 quart	32 fl. oz.	1 L
1 gallon	128 fl. oz.	4 L

Weight Equivalents

US Standard	Metric (approximate)
1 ounce	28 g
2 ounces	57 g
5 ounces	142 g
10 ounces	284 g
15 ounces	425 g
16 ounces (1 pound)	455 g
1.5 pounds	680 g
2 pounds	907 g

Temperature Equivalents

Fahrenheit (F)	Celsius (C) approximate
225 °F	107 °C
250 °F	120 °
275 °F	135 °C
300 °F	150 °C
325 °F	160 °C
350 °F	180 °C
375 °F	190 °C
400 °F	205 °C
425 °F	220 °C
450 °F	235 °C
475 °F	245 °C
500 °F	260 °C

DIRTY DOZEN & CLEAN FIFTEEN

The Galveston Diet emphasizes whole, nutrient-dense foods to support hormone balance and overall health. However, the quality of the produce you choose is just as important as the type. The Environmental Working Group (EWG) annually publishes the Dirty Dozen and Clean Fifteen lists, which highlight the most and least pesticide-contaminated fruits and vegetables. These lists are based on rigorous analysis of testing data from the U.S. Department of Agriculture (USDA) and the U.S. Food and Drug Administration (FDA). For 2024, the EWG examined 47,510 samples of 46 fruits and vegetables to determine pesticide residue levels.

THE DIRTY DOZEN

Pesticides, especially fungicides like fludioxonil and pyrimethanil, are commonly found on conventional produce and are known for their potential to disrupt the endocrine system, which can impact hormonal health—a key focus of the Galveston Diet. These chemicals can accumulate in the body, potentially leading to negative health effects, including impacts on reproductive health.
The EWG's analysis found that 75 percent of all conventional fresh produce samples contained pesticide residues, with the Dirty Dozen showing contamination in 95 percent of samples. Here are the most pesticide-laden fruits and vegetables that made the Dirty Dozen list for 2024:

The Dirty Dozen	
Strawberries	Nectarines
Spinach	Apples
Kale, collard, and mustard greens	Bell and hot peppers
Grapes	Cherries
Peaches	Blueberries
Pears	Green beans

THE CLEAN FIFTEEN

For those on the Galveston Diet, choosing produce with lower pesticide levels can be beneficial. The Clean Fifteen list identifies fruits and vegetables that have the lowest pesticide residues, making them safer choices even when conventionally grown. Nearly 65 percent of samples on the Clean Fifteen had no detectable pesticide residues.

Here are the Clean Fifteen for 2024:

The Clean Fifteen	
Avocados	Kiwi
Sweet corn	Cabbage
Pineapple	Watermelon
Onions	Mushrooms
Sweet peas (frozen)	Mangoes
Papaya	Sweet potatoes
Asparagus	Carrots
Honeydew melon	

Recommendations for the Galveston Diet

For those following the Galveston Diet, EWG recommends prioritizing organic versions of items on the Dirty Dozen list to reduce pesticide exposure, while both organic and conventional versions of Clean Fifteen produce are generally considered safe.

However, it's worth noting that some industry groups challenge the EWG's findings. Organizations like the Alliance for Food and Farming argue that the pesticide levels in conventionally grown produce are generally too low to pose significant health risks and emphasize that the health benefits of consuming more fruits and vegetables outweigh the potential risks from pesticides. They also suggest that thorough washing can effectively reduce pesticide residues.

 NOTES

....

....

....

....

....

....

....

....

....

....

....

....

....

....

....

....

....

....

 NOTES

THANK YOU FOR READING!

As an independent author with a limited marketing budget, reviews are essential for my success on Amazon platform. If you liked this book, I would be so grateful if you could share your honest thoughts!

Feel free to click the QR code below to get started! It's always a joy to hear from my readers, and I make it a point to read each and every review myself.

Made in the USA
Monee, IL
21 November 2024

70697611R00063